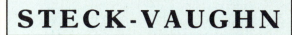

STECK-VAUGHN
GED

SOCIAL STUDIES
Geography
History
Political Science
Economics
Behavioral Science

Susan D. McClanahan, Educational Consultant
Donna D. Amstutz, Special Advisor

STECK-VAUGHN ADULT EDUCATION ADVISORY COUNCIL

Donna D. Amstutz
Asst. Project Director
Northern Area Adult Education
 Service Center
Northern Illinois University
DeKalb, Illinois

Lonnie D. Farrell
Supervisor, Adult Special Programs
Los Angeles Unified School District
Los Angeles, California

Meredyth A. Leahy
Director of Continuing
 Education
Cabrini College
Radnor, Pennsylvania

Roberta Pittman
Director, Project C3 Adult Basic
 Education
Detroit Public Schools
Detroit, Michigan

Don F. Seaman
Professor, Adult Education
College of Education
Texas A&M University
College Station, Texas

Jane B. Sellen
Supervisor, Adult Education
Western Iowa Tech
 Community College
Sioux City, Iowa

Elaine Shelton
Consultant, Competency-Based
 Adult Education
Austin, Texas

Bobbie L. Walden
Coordinator, Community Education
Alabama Department of Education
Montgomery, Alabama

Steck-Vaughn
Company

A Subsidiary of National Education Corporation

Product Design and Development: McClanahan & Company
with PC&F, Inc.

Project Director: Bonnie Diamond, Ed. D.

Assistant Project Director: Patricia Carlin

Design/Production Director: Judi Baller

Editorial Development: Bette Kalash, Ph. D., Lisa Greenberg,
Patricia Parmalee, Winifred Davis

ISBN 0-8114-1896-0   3 4 5 6 7 8 9 0 PO 91 90 89 88

Contents

To the Student

The GED test offers you an opportunity to

1. Keep or get a better job in government, industry or business
2. Increase your earning powers
3. Expand educational opportunities in trade, technical, vocational, or apprenticeship programs
4. Fulfill your personal goals

It awards a certificate that is the equivalent of a high school diploma. It measures your mastery of skills and general knowledge in Writing Skills, Social Studies, Science, Reading Literature and the Arts, and Mathematics.

The Steck-Vaughn program prepares you for success on the GED exam by:

- Teaching appropriate concepts and skills that will provide a solid foundation for your general knowledge
- Providing practice in the GED format
- Emphasizing the reading skills that will be tested on the GED exam—those that require you to apply, to analyze and to evaluate as well as to comprehend what you read
- Offering test-taking tips to build your confidence
- Applying concepts and skills in practical and realistic settings
- Building vocabulary by highlighting and defining new terms
- Teaching reading, writing and problem-solving skills to make you better readers
- Frequently using charts, tables, graphs, diagrams, maps and figures, which are part of the GED test, and instructing you how to gain meaning from them.

It does this through an easy-to-follow, predictable Four Step Plan that includes

- Introducing and teaching a concept
- Applying a particular reading or problem-solving strategy to the concept
- Practicing the concept in the GED test format
- Testing and checking your answers

(Answers and Explanations to both the Practice and GED Mini-Test items provide further instruction through explanations of why choices are incorrect as well as why a given choice is correct.)

The following table summarizes the contents of the GED tests.

The Tests of General Educational Development

Test	Content Areas	Number of Items	Time Limit (minutes)
Writing Skills	PART ONE Sentence Structure Usage Mechanics	55	75
Writing Sample	PART TWO Essay	1	45
Social Studies	United States History Geography Economics Political Science Behavioral Science	64	85
Science	Life Science Earth Science Physics Chemistry	66	95
Reading Literature and the Arts	Popular Literature Classical Literature Commentary	45	65
Mathematics	Arithmetic Measurement Number Relationships Data Analysis Algebra Geometry	56	90

How To Use This Book

The Book

A sequentially organized program

The Pretest

- Tells you what content and skills you have already mastered and
- What content and skills you need to work on—a real aid to planning your time and increasing your studying efficiency
  (See the Pretest/Posttest Diagnostic Chart in the back of this book)

The Overview

- Explains each major section of the book
- Provides definitions of vocabulary terms and concepts that relate to material in each major section

The Study Plan

 a practical reminder when applying a concept

 a practical reminder related to test-taking

A predictable seven-page lesson that includes:

- An **Introductory** teaching page
- A **Strategy** page that teaches and applies a related reading skill to increase understanding and aid mastery
- **Practice** pages that review and reinforce the particular content and the reading skill in GED format
- **Mixed Practice** exercises in the Mathematics and Writing texts that review previously learned material
- A multiple choice, GED format test (**GED Mini-Test**) that measures higher-level thinking skills
- **Answers and Explanations** for both the Practice and the GED Mini-Tests that give *immediate* feedback and pinpoint possible errors or weaknesses

The Review

- Summarizes the instructional content of a section
- Provides more practice items in GED format

The Posttest

- Simulates the actual GED test
- Alerts you to the need for possible further study
  (See the Pretest/Posttest Diagnostic Chart in the back of this book)

Test-Taking and Study Skills

Test-Taking Skills

The *AIM* of the Steck-Vaughn GED program is to prepare you to take and to pass the GED examination with ease and confidence. You bring to the program your own personal style and your life experience.

With these as a base, use the preparation material and the suggestions that follow to build and strengthen your academic skills, test-taking ability and study skills.

The Steck-Vaughn program is designed to provide numerous test taking situations in the multiple-choice GED format. GED items appear in:

- Pre- and posttests for each book
- Practice and test pages for each lesson
- Reviews for each major book section

The more opportunities you have to practice the GED test format, the more you will increase your confidence in test taking. *You learn about the test by preparing for the test.*

Some key test-taking skills are:

- Set goals
- Plan your test-taking time
- Read for understanding
- Analyze the test questions carefully before answering them
- Pace yourself

Reviewing the helpful Steck-Vaughn GED Mini-Test Tips that are part of each lesson will help you gain more confidence in test taking.

Study Skills

The Steck-Vaughn program aids in developing and improving your study skills. They are an important element in successful test taking.

Some important study skills to remember are

- Improve your vocabulary
- Use your text as well as other resources, including maps, charts, graphs and diagrams to help you learn
- Plan your study time
- Take notes and use your notes to study from; your notes can be a map or an outline or any form that is most helpful for you
- Make a check-list of the areas that give you trouble and refer to this list so you practice what is difficult for you
- Problem solve:
  - discover what the problem (question) is
  - list two or three possible solutions
  - choose the one best answer
  - try it out
  - re-think and research if it does not work.

Try to find out why a solution is wrong and keep that in mind to apply to future material you read.

The on-going repetition and review of both the test-taking and study skill strategies and the constant practice will give you confidence and self-assurance as you prepare for and take the GED exam.

PRETEST
Social Studies

DIRECTIONS: Choose the one best answer for each item below.

Items 1–4 refer to the following passage.

Thomas Paine's short pamphlet *Common Sense* encouraged many colonial Americans to support the idea of revolution against Great Britain. He wrote:

"I have heard it asserted by some, that as America has flourished under her former connection with Great Britain, the same connection is necessary toward her future happiness, and will always have the same effect. Nothing can be more fallacious than this kind of argument. We may as well assert that because a child has thrived upon milk, that it is never to have meat, or that the first twenty years of our lives is to become a precedent for the next twenty. But even this is admitting more than is true; for I answer roundly, that America would have flourished as much, and probably much more, had no European power taken any notice of her. The commerce by which she hath enriched herself are the necessaries of life, and will always have a market while eating is the custom of Europe."

1. Which of the following is the *best* summary of Paine's argument in the paragraph?

    (1) Children need milk in order to live.
    (2) What was good in the past is good for the future.
    (3) America will thrive on neglect; it does not need Europe.
    (4) America's greatest resource is its abundance of raw materials.
    (5) America's growth stems from its own resources, not from Great Britain's support.

2. Paine states that the argument that America has flourished and will continue to flourish under Great Britain is fallacious, or false. He shows that the argument is false by

    (1) the example of changes in eating habits as a child grows
    (2) posing a series of unanswerable riddles
    (3) demonstrating that America could be economically independent
    (4) demonstrating that America could be economically self-sufficient
    (5) admitting that the argument is more than true

3. Americans tend to have an idealistic streak. To which of the following American ideals or values does Paine's writing appeal?

    (1) life
    (2) liberty
    (3) the pursuit of happiness
    (4) equality
    (5) religious freedom

4. Great Britain thought that the American colonies existed only to benefit Great Britain, the home country. Paine's paragraph implies that that benefit was primarily

    (1) political
    (2) military
    (3) economic
    (4) social
    (5) religious

GO ON TO THE NEXT PAGE.

Items 5–10 refer to the following definitions.

Man is set apart from other creatures by his ability to learn and to integrate new experiences with old experiences. Psychologists have formulated many theories and principles of learning to explain how man learns. Five of these are described below:

(1) Positive transfer—earlier learning facilitates or makes easier the learning of new skills or material

(2) Negative transfer—earlier learning interferes with, or makes difficult, the learning of new skills or material

(3) Cognitive dissonance—new facts contradict earlier learning and are avoided or ignored

(4) Cognitive consonance—new facts agree with earlier learning and are retained and accepted

(5) Reinforcement—learning that is rewarded either internally through self-satisfaction or externally by social approval or valued tokens will be encouraged and repeated.

5. A confirmed smoker sees a newspaper headline saying "American Medical Association Study Denies that Smoking is Linked to Early Death." She cuts the article out to show her husband, who is trying to get her to stop smoking. This is an example of

(1) positive transfer
(2) negative transfer
(3) cognitive dissonance
(4) cognitive consonance
(5) reinforcement

6. A teacher has many disruptive behavior problems in her classroom. She agrees with the class that she will award a gold star to the class for every ten minutes of quiet working and cooperation. For ten gold stars the class will have an extra ten minutes of recess time. This teacher is using

(1) positive transfer
(2) negative transfer
(3) cognitive dissonance
(4) cognitive consonance
(5) reinforcement

7. During the Vietnam War, some American soldiers were involved in torturing and killing Vietnamese civilians. When these incidents were first reported in the press, many Americans refused to believe the reports. They thought that American soldiers were brave and moral men. This is an example of

(1) positive transfer
(2) negative transfer
(3) cognitive dissonance
(4) cognitive consonance
(5) reinforcement

8. An American with a background in labor organizing work is accepted into the Peace Corps. She is asked to supervise a fishing cooperative in Guatemala. She finds that her former work with labor unions makes it easy for her to communicate the practical advantages of a cooperative to Guatemalan fishermen. She is receiving the benefits of

(1) positive transfer
(2) negative transfer
(3) cognitive dissonance
(4) cognitive consonance
(5) reinforcement

GO ON TO THE NEXT PAGE.

9. A clerical worker is asked to switch from one word processing system to another with a different keyboard and different commands. Despite a short training course, the worker constantly touches the wrong keys on the keyboard. The clerk is suffering the effects of

(1) positive transfer
(2) negative transfer
(3) cognitive dissonance
(4) cognitive consonance
(5) reinforcement

10. A mother who has stayed home for many years to bring up her three children decides to re-enter the work force. On her first job she finds that the people in her office seem to be working against each other. She uses some of the techniques she used with her children to encourage cooperation among her co-workers. This is an example of

(1) positive transfer
(2) negative transfer
(3) cognitive dissonance
(4) cognitive consonance
(5) reinforcement

11. In the United States many corporations issue stock to shareholders in exchange for money to pay for the activities of the corporation. The shareholders are the owners of the corporation. However, the corporation is run by the management, which may own as little as 1% of the stock. This leads to a separation of ownership and control in large corporations. One probable result is

(1) owners having little control over their companies
(2) management acting on the behalf of itself
(3) management becoming incompetent
(4) owners selling the stock that they own
(5) bankruptcy of the corporation

12. Laissez-faire in economics means a government attitude of non-interference in economic affairs. The government intervenes only to maintain property rights. Which of the following is an example of laissez-faire?

(1) import tariffs
(2) sales taxes
(3) export quotas
(4) farmer's market
(5) parity pricing of farm products

13. A monopoly occurs when one company has the exclusive ownership or control of a good or service. A monopoly has the power to set prices as it wishes since no other company can provide the product or service. In 1890 the Sherman Antitrust Act was passed. It stated that a business monopoly "in restraint of trade or commerce" was illegal. Which of the following is the *best* reason for the passage of the Sherman Antitrust Act?

(1) Monopolies were good for the country's economy.
(2) Monopolies prevented the working of a free and open market.
(3) In 1890 the country was suffering from too many high prices.
(4) Exclusive ownership is against the American ideals of liberty and independence for all.
(5) Monopolies made their owners too rich.

14. Many underdeveloped countries wish to pursue the goal of economic development. They would like to be numbered among the rich instead of the poor. Four factors key to development are population, natural resources, creation of capital or money and development of technology. What would an underdeveloped country do about population in order to speed economic development?

(1) campaign to have larger families
(2) convince citizens to limit the size of their families
(3) start nutrition programs
(4) encourage emigration into the country
(5) begin a socialized medicine and health program

GO ON TO THE NEXT PAGE.

15. An individual's discretionary income is income that is not used to pay for the necessities of life: food, clothing, shelter and so on. If housing costs go up, what will be the effect on discretionary income for an individual?

    (1) Discretionary income will be used to pay for housing.
    (2) Discretionary income will be increased.
    (3) The individual will demand a pay raise.
    (4) The individual will revise his household budget.
    (5) Discretionary income will be decreased.

16. The threat of international terrorism has exerted an economic effect on the world. The *most* likely economic effect of a spate of airline hijackings and bombings is

    (1) less tourism
    (2) more tourism
    (3) airlines going out of business
    (4) closing of airports
    (5) increased airport security

17. Insurance companies usually adjust their rates for different age and sex groups depending on general characteristics of the group. For example, young men between ages 18 and 24 usually have the highest proportion of traffic accidents in the population. Consequently, their car insurance rates are the highest. Many insurance companies adjust their rates downward for teenagers who have had driver's education. Insurance companies will increase rates for individuals who have been involved in traffic accidents. Which of the following people would have the *lowest* car insurance rate?

    (1) a teenage boy who took driver's education
    (2) a teenage boy who did not take driver's education
    (3) a teenage girl who took driver's education
    (4) a teenage girl who did not take driver's education
    (5) a 23-year-old man with one traffic accident.

18. Terrorism is the use of terror as a political weapon. Violent acts are used to coerce governments to comply with terrorist demands. Most acts of terrorism now stem from conflicts in the Middle East. However, the United States is the target of about a third of the terrorist incidents worldwide. Often terrorists operate in countries other than their own. Which of the following acts of violence could *not* be described as an act of terrorism?

    (1) A Lebanese guerilla drives a truck armed with explosives into the American embassy in Beirut.
    (2) An Irish girl, at the request of her Syrian boyfriend, carries a package of explosives onto a Pan Am airplane.
    (3) The American ambassador to Afghanistan is abducted and shot in a hotel.
    (4) A peaceful protester is critically injured in a demonstration against nuclear power plants in North Dakota.
    (5) A Greek cruise ship is hijacked in the Mediterranean and an American is shot.

19. In large corporations middle management often reaches a bottleneck in promotions. Very few reach senior executive positions. Affirmative action programs in the 1970s and 1980s concentrated on encouraging corporations to offer jobs to blacks and women. Between 1985 and 1995 blacks and women will account for 75% of the growth in the labor force. On what will affirmative action programs *most* likely focus?

    (1) entry-level jobs
    (2) higher wages
    (3) blue-collar jobs
    (4) American Indian employment
    (5) upward job mobility

20. The Great Atlantic and Pacific Tea Company, which owns the A&P grocery store chain, was taken over by a German company and revived by an English executive. The Japanese have cornered 10% of the U.S. dried soup market in just a few years. American food imports are rapidly growing while exports are decreasing. These are *all* indications of

    (1) the internationalization of the U.S.
    (2) dependence on foreign expertise
    (3) growth of national pride and privilege
    (4) internationalization of the American food industry
    (5) the rising commercialism of Japan

GO ON TO THE NEXT PAGE.

Items 21–23 refer to the following table.

MAJOR WORLD FOOD PRODUCTION (averages for 1979–81)

Meat
- United States 17.5%
- China 16.0%
- U.S.S.R. 11.0%
- France 3.8%

Rice
- China 36.6%
- India 6.8%
- Bangladesh 5.0%
- Thailand 4.0%

Corn
- United States 45.8%
- China 14.5%
- Brazil 4.5%
- Mexico 2.8%

Potato
- U.S.S.R. 29.8%
- Poland 15.5%
- United States 5.8%
- China 5.8%

Wheat
- U.S.S.R. 20.7%
- United States 20.0%
- China 13.0%
- India 7.7%

Soybean
- United States 64%
- Brazil 15.1%
- China 10.5%
- Argentina 4.7%

21. Before a country can export food to other countries it must first feed its own people. China, with one quarter of the people in the world, is the single country with the largest population. The table indicates that the *largest* exporter of food in the world is probably

(1) Brazil
(2) China
(3) India
(4) U.S.A.
(5) U.S.S.R.

22. From information in the table what can be predicted about the American diet compared to the diet of the rest of the world? Americans eat

(1) more potatoes
(2) a more vegetarian diet
(3) less meat
(4) more meat
(5) less food

23. China has one-quarter of the world's population. What can be inferred about China's food imports and exports?

(1) China exports meat and imports fish.
(2) China imports meat and exports fish.
(3) China exports rice and imports wheat.
(4) China imports rice and exports wheat.
(5) China is self-sufficient in food.

24. **Vegetarianism** is the practice of living on a diet of vegetables, grains and fruits. This is sometimes supplemented by milk or eggs, but meat is never eaten. Some people adhere to vegetarianism because of a religious or philosophical belief. Others follow vegetarianism because they believe that it can keep more people in the world fed. With the information that four to five pounds of grain are used to produce one pound of beef, how could a vegetarian support his theory about feeding the starving people of the world?

(1) Not producing 140 million metric tons of meat would increase grain production by at least 560 million metric tons.
(2) Not producing 140 million metric tons of meat would release 560 million metric tons of grain for human consumption.
(3) It is healthier to eat grain products and everyone should do it.
(4) The fat in meat causes clogging of the arteries and increases the probability of heart attacks.
(5) The real problem is getting the food to the people who need it, so it does not matter what sort of food it is.

GO ON TO THE NEXT PAGE.

Items 25–26 refer to the following cartoon.

"Liberals!"

25. What does this cartoon indicate about the liberal and his political attitudes?

    (1) Liberals are too realistic.
    (2) Liberals want to help everyone.
    (3) Liberals are for the birds.
    (4) Liberals make good neighbors.
    (5) Liberals feed the birds in winter.

26. What does the cartoon indicate about the speaker in the picture?

    (1) He is a liberal.
    (2) He is a radical.
    (3) He is a businessman.
    (4) He likes liberals.
    (5) He dislikes liberals.

Answers and Explanations

Social Studies Pretest   *pp. 4–9*

1. **Answer:** (5) This is correct because Paine rejects the argument for historical precedence and then makes the point that America flourishes through its own resources and might have done better without any support from Europe at all. Choice (1) is an example to support an argument. Choice (2) is the opposite of one point that Paine makes. Choice (3) is an opinion of Paine's. Choice (4) is information not included in the paragraph.

2. **Answer:** (1) This is correct because Paine is comparing a child's eating habits to America's connection to Great Britain. As a child grows, he changes from a protected diet of his mother's milk to an independent diet of meat that he chews by himself; as America grows, it should be able to change from a status of being protected as a colony to a status of political independence as a separate country, able to deal with its own problems in its own way.

3. **Answer:** (2) This is correct because Paine is arguing against America's "former connection," or alliance, with Great Britain as a colonial empire. He is encouraging his fellow Americans to break the connection with Great Britain and assert their independence and freedom.

4. **Answer:** (3) This is correct because Paine states that America has enriched itself through the commerce of the necessities of life, particularly food.

5. **Answer:** (4) This is correct because the smoker finds information that agrees with her prior learning or attitudes and accepts that information because it supports her cognitive structure.

6. **Answer:** (5) This is correct because the teacher is using rewards, or reinforcement, to encourage the learning of a new behavior pattern.

7. **Answer:** (3) This is correct because the example describes a situation of rejection of information because it does not fit with prior beliefs and attitudes.

8. **Answer:** (1) This is correct because the individual is transferring her former knowledge of how to work with laborers to a new situation of working with Guatemalan fishermen.

9. **Answer:** (2) This is correct because prior learning is interfering with new learning.

10. **Answer:** (1) This is correct because the mother is using her learning about group behavior in the family to encourage cooperation in a new group in the work place.

11. **Answer:** (1) This is correct because the management that runs the company may own little of the stock, while the stockholders who own most of the company have little say in the management of the corporation because their ownership is so diluted.

12. **Answer:** (4) This is correct because it is the only example in which the government plays no part. Choices (1) to (3) and (5) are all examples of government interference in or regulation of the economy.

13. **Answer:** (2) This is correct by reasoning from the definition. A monopoly can set prices as high as it likes because no other company can provide the product or the service. Therefore, it restrains trade by interfering with the workings of an open market in which the market or demand sets the price. Choices (1) and (4) are false. Choice (3) may or may not be true; no information is given. Choice (5) is an opinion.

14. **Answer:** (2) This is correct because most underdeveloped countries have populations too large for their natural resources and technology to support. Therefore, by limiting the population the government can distribute its resources to satisfy the needs of its citizens and can increase the resources dedicated to development. Choices (1) and (4) would increase the problem for most countries. Choice (3) would not take care of the problem of insufficient resources. Choice (5) would take additional government resources that most underdeveloped countries do not have.

15. **Answer:** (5) This is correct because if housing prices go up, more of an individual's income is dedicated to basic needs and less is available for non-necessities. Choice (1) contradicts the definition of discretionary income. Choice (2) is the opposite of what will happen. Choices (3) and (4) are not effects on discretionary income.

16. **Answer:** (1) This is correct because it is an economic effect that follows from the fears of travelers. Choice (2) is incorrect because people will not willingly put themselves in dangerous situations. Choices (3) and (4) are too exaggerated; airlines will adapt by decreasing the number of flights to suit the smaller market of travelers, and airports will, likewise, adjust to a smaller market of commercial travelers. Choice (5) is a probable effect, but it is not economic.

17. **Answer:** (3) This is correct by a careful reading of the answers. Each answer must be compared to the information in the paragraph. Males in the given age group have higher rates, so choices (1), (2) and (5) are eliminated. Those without driver's education have higher rates, so choice (4) is eliminated.

18. **Answer:** (4) This is correct because the protester is not acting in a violent manner. Instead the paragraph states that the action is peaceful, although politically directed.

19. **Answer:** (5) This is correct because the estimated growth of the numbers of blacks and women in the work force will take care of the entry level jobs, choice (1). However, blacks and women who entered the job market in the 1970s and 1980s will be caught in the corporate bottleneck, so affirmative action programs will concentrate on getting blacks and women into higher management positions with more authority.

20. **Answer:** (4) Choice (1) is too general. Choice (2) does not cover the information about imports and exports. Choice (3) is irrelevant. Choice (5) relates to only one sentence in the paragraph.

21. **Answer:** (4) This is correct because the U.S.A. is the major or a major producer in each category except rice. Choice (1), Brazil, is a major producer of only corn and soybeans. Choice (2), China, which is mentioned in every category, only exceeds the percentage of its population in its production of rice. Choice (3), India, is a major producer of only rice and wheat, and, from general knowledge, has an enormous population. Choice (5), the U.S.S.R., is a major producer in only three out of six categories.

22. **Answer:** (4) Americans produce more meat so probably eat more meat because it is available. While it also produces more corn and soybeans, those products are used primarily as food for cattle and pigs. Choice (1) is inaccurate because the U.S.S.R. and Polish diets probably include more potatoes than the American diet. Choice (3) is the opposite of the logical prediction. Choice (5) is inaccurate because the U.S. produces so much more food than other countries.

23. **Answer:** (3) This is correct given the information that China has 25% of the people, produces 36% of the rice (about 11% more than it needs, assuming equal distribution of the world's resources) and produces 13% of the wheat (about half of what it needs).

24. **Answer:** (2) This is correct because not feeding the grain products to animals would make them available to human beings. Choice (1) is wrong because the grain production would not be increased; present grain production would be redistributed. Choices (3) and (4) are not mentioned in the information given. Choice (5) is an argument that would not support vegetarianism.

25. **Answer:** (2) This is correct because the food in the birdhouse is available to both squirrels and birds. Most bird feeders are designed to prevent squirrels from sharing the bird seed.

26. **Answer:** (5) This is correct from the expression on the speaker's face, which is negative.

To figure out your score, count the problems you missed. Then subtract the number of problems you missed from the total number of questions on the test. If half or more are correct, you may consider that you have passed the test. To organize your study time efficiently, turn to the Pretest/Posttest Diagnostic Chart in the back of this book.

OVERVIEW
Geography

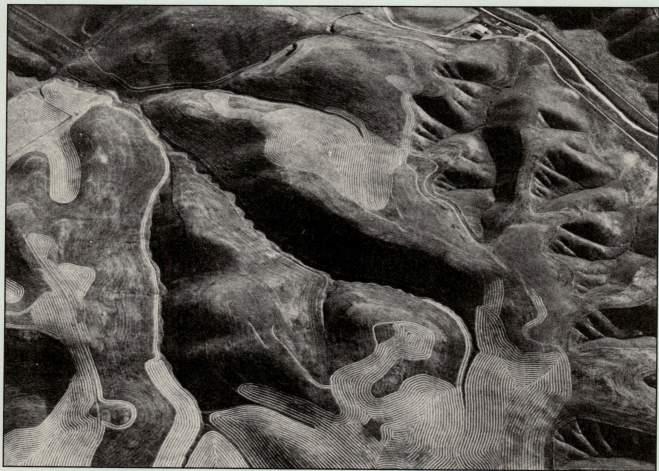

Barley fields of Paso Robles, California, after the harvest.

map
representation on flat surface of all or part of an area

globe
spherical representation of the earth

Geography studies three main topics:

1. Physical elements of the world like water, landforms, soils, mineral resources, plant and animal life and climate
2. How physical elements in an area define culture and society
3. How humans affect the physical world

The physical world can be shown on a **map,** a two-dimensional picture of our three-dimensional world, or a **globe,** a three-dimensional replica of the world. Many different kinds of maps are designed to communicate different ideas. The most common types of maps are political, physical and special purpose.

Political maps show regional borders, which are political (man-made) divisions. They may indicate capital cities, major highways, waterways and so forth. Heavy black lines usually indicate borders while contrasting colors differentiate bordering regions. See page 14 for an example of a political map.

Physical maps represent the physical attributes of an area. They may include lakes, rivers, mountains, plateaus and coasts. These characteristics may be used to show variations in climate, sites of natural resources, geographical changes through history and so forth. See page 14 for an example of a physical map.

Special purpose maps demonstrate a particular idea. They may give information on how humans affect the environment by industrialization or how the environment affects humans by determining trade routes and population dispersion in a particular area, and even how humans and the environment interact, as in a map showing types of pollution. See page 15 for an example of a special purpose map.

Common elements that a **cartographer**, or map-maker, uses to draw maps are a **title**, which indicates the main idea of a map; a **legend**, which represents specific symbolic or coded information such as elevation, railroads, natural resources and so forth; a **compass rose**, which shows direction; a map **scale**, which shows distance on the map compared to distance in the real world. Distance is measured in inches/miles or centimeters/kilometers.

Lines of latitude and longitude are used to help locate a specific area. **Longitude lines** run north-south, the "long" way between the poles, and are always the same in length. **Latitude lines** run parallel to the **Equator**, and get shorter as they approach the poles.

legend
explanatory list, sometimes pictorial, of the symbols on a map

compass rose
direction guide; lists the cardinal direction points: North, South, East, West. North is always at the top

Equator
imaginary line, equidistant from the two poles; divides the earth into the northern and southern hemispheres

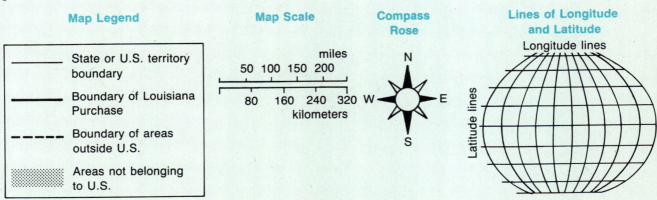

Map Legend

———— State or U.S. territory boundary

———— Boundary of Louisiana Purchase

- - - - - Boundary of areas outside U.S.

▒▒▒▒ Areas not belonging to U.S.

Map Scale

miles
50 100 150 200

80   160   240 320
kilometers

Compass Rose

N
W — E
S

Lines of Longitude and Latitude

Longitude lines

Latitude lines

Earth's Regions I

The United States and Canada are two adjoining countries that make up a large part of the continent of North America. Their histories have intertwined since pre-colonial days. Both countries are as diverse as they are large. Their geography has had an enormous impact on their history. The maps below give varying amounts of different information. Information not given outright can be deduced.

The states and provinces of the United States and Canada share many common borders.

One of the states (Alaska) is separated from the **contiguous** (touching) United States by thousands of miles. Without friendly relationships between governments, this physical layout could lead to border disputes or war.

Since this has not been the case between the two countries since the War of 1812, it can be assumed that relationships between the two countries today are friendly.

Study the physical and political maps below. Compare them to the special purpose map on page 15.

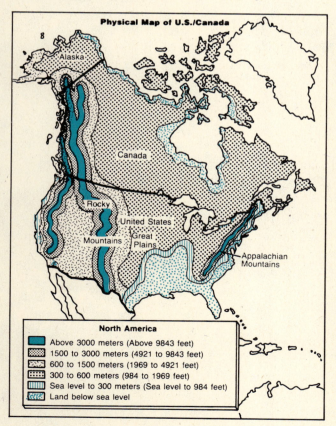

Physical Map of U.S./Canada

North America

- ■ Above 3000 meters (Above 9843 feet)
- ▨ 1500 to 3000 meters (4921 to 9843 feet)
- ▨ 600 to 1500 meters (1969 to 4921 feet)
- ▨ 300 to 600 meters (984 to 1969 feet)
- ▥ Sea level to 300 meters (Sea level to 984 feet)
- ▨ Land below sea level

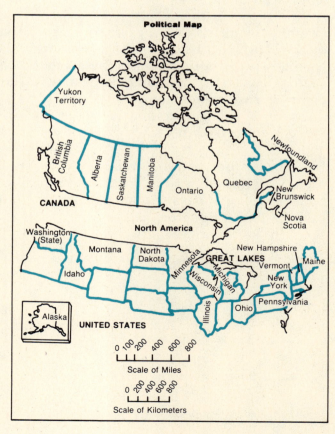

Political Map

Scale of Miles
0 100 200 400 600 800

Scale of Kilometers
0 200 400 600 800

═══ Restate Information ═══

This skill involves identifying the main idea and supporting details of a map in order to present information in another way. It can help you better understand something you are reading or studying.

This special purpose map shows the same area as the maps on page 14, but the information differs. *Read the title* for the *main idea.* Read the legend for **supporting details.** To answer the following question, **restate information.**

How is the Spanish influence in North America seen today? Is it through

(1) dress   (2) inventory units
(3) education   (4) place names
(5) farming techniques

The legend tells you that the Spanish claimed the territories shown with colored dots. In that area, the Rio Grande and Colorado rivers, and Sante Fe, have Spanish names. The **answer** is choice (4).

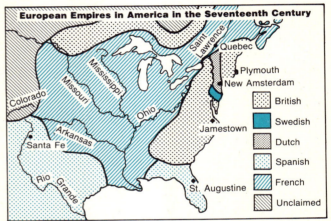

European Empires in America in the Seventeenth Century

Legend:
- British
- Swedish
- Dutch
- Spanish
- French
- Unclaimed

Examples

DIRECTIONS: Choose the <u>one</u> best answer for each item below.

Item 1 refers to the political map and item 2 refers to the physical map on page 14.

1. A modern concern involving both Canada and the United States would *most* likely be

   (1) education
   (2) water pollution
   (3) the space race
   (4) political corruption
   (5) taxes

Answer: (2) Although the other four choices are concerns to many governments, water pollution is a joint concern because of the shared land mass.

2. Which area of both countries is *least* suitable for farming?

   (1) Northwest
   (2) Southeast
   (3) Northeast
   (4) Eastern Seaboard
   (5) South

Answer: (1) The Rocky Mountains extend from New Mexico, through Canada, into Alaska. Mountainous terrain is not good for farming.

> *Rephrase* the map's main idea in your own words. For example, "Indian Population and Migration in 1800" might be restated as "Where certain Indians moved to in the 1800s."

DIRECTIONS: Choose the <u>one</u> best answer for each item below.

Items 1–4 refer to the following map.

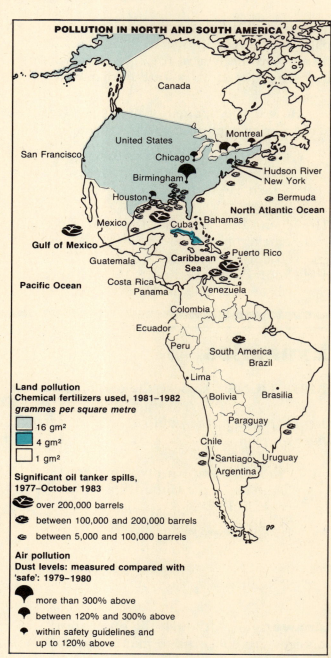

POLLUTION IN NORTH AND SOUTH AMERICA

Land pollution
Chemical fertilizers used, 1981–1982
grammes per square metre

- ▢ 16 gm²
- ▢ 4 gm²
- ▢ 1 gm²

Significant oil tanker spills, 1977–October 1983

- over 200,000 barrels
- between 100,000 and 200,000 barrels
- between 5,000 and 100,000 barrels

Air pollution
Dust levels: measured compared with 'safe': 1979–1980

- more than 300% above
- between 120% and 300% above
- within safety guidelines and up to 120% above

1. A person who suffered from dust allergies would *not* choose to live in

   (1) San Francisco, California
   (2) Birmingham, Alabama
   (3) Brasilia, Brazil
   (4) Lima, Peru
   (5) Santiago, Chile

2. The most severe damage to ocean life (due to oil spills) in U.S. coastal waters during 1977–1983 took place in the

   (1) Pacific Ocean
   (2) North Atlantic Ocean
   (3) Gulf of Mexico
   (4) Caribbean Sea
   (5) Hudson River

3. The use of chemical fertilizers is

   (1) greater in Argentina than in Canada
   (2) greater in Canada than in Brazil
   (3) greater in the U.S. than in Canada
   (4) less in the U.S. than in Canada
   (5) less in Mexico than in Colombia

4. Given the hypothesis that more economically developed countries have higher levels of pollution, which country would have the highest standard of living?

   (1) Argentina
   (2) Brazil
   (3) Cuba
   (4) United States
   (5) Canada

GO ON TO THE NEXT PAGE.

Items 5–6 refer to the following passage.

Many scientists are concerned about a shift in world temperature known as the "greenhouse effect." The atmosphere seems to be getting warmer every year. Scientists wonder if atmospheric heating and cooling is a repeated phenomenon, or if this warming up of the earth's atmosphere is a unique occurrence.

One explanation for the atmospheric warm-up is the disappearance of tropical rain forests in Latin America and Africa. As countries in South America and Africa have developed, they have cut down forests in order to expand their agricultural and industrial economies. Some scientists think deforestation has led to an increase of nitric oxide, a destroyer of the ozone layer.

5. Which statement is *not* based on information given in the passage?

(1) Scientists are worried about the "greenhouse effect."
(2) The earth's atmosphere has heated up before.
(3) Deforestation might be a cause of increased nitric oxide.
(4) There are several possible explanations of the "greenhouse effect."
(5) Poor countries sometimes sacrifice conservation for development.

Items 7–10 refer to the following map.

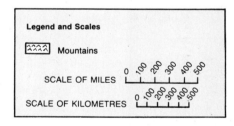

6. Which two groups would *most* likely band together to prevent deforestation?

(1) conservationists and atmospheric scientists
(2) politicians and greenhouse builders
(3) economic developers and farmers
(4) farmers and conservationists
(5) atmospheric scientists and greenhouse builders

7. The Western European country *most* unlikely to support a navy would be

(1) England
(2) Italy
(3) Netherlands
(4) Spain
(5) Switzerland

8. The Netherlands, a low-lying area, is *most* prone to

(1) invasions
(2) poor farming conditions
(3) flooding from the sea
(4) lack of tourism
(5) mass immigration

9. Which country is bordered on all sides by mountains and seas?

(1) Ireland
(2) Italy
(3) France
(4) Scotland
(5) Spain

Before you take the GED Mini-Test, check your answers on page 19.

GED Mini-Test

TIP 1

As you take a GED Mini-Test, relax. Remember it is designed to help you build your confidence in test taking. Set your goals for this test. Then use the Answers and Explanations to analyze how you did.

MIDDLE EASTERN OIL PRODUCTION

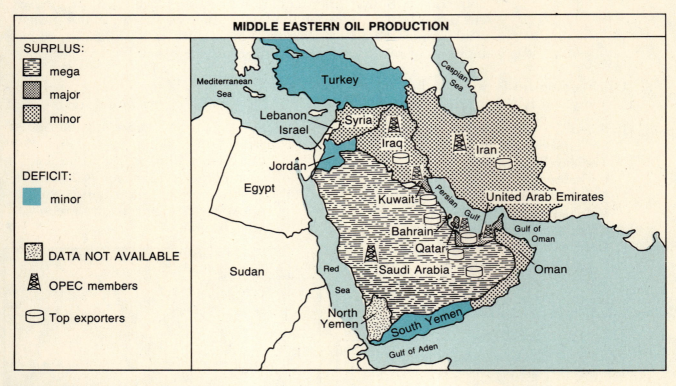

SURPLUS:

- mega
- major
- minor

DEFICIT:

- minor

- DATA NOT AVAILABLE
- OPEC members
- Top exporters

DIRECTIONS: Choose the one best answer for each item below.

Items 1–6 refer to the above map.

1. Which Middle Eastern country is the largest exporter of oil?

   (1) Bahrain
   (2) Iran
   (3) Iraq
   (4) Saudi Arabia
   (5) United Arab Emirates

2. According to the map, which of the following countries would have the poorest, least developed economy?

   (1) Iran
   (2) Iraq
   (3) Kuwait
   (4) Saudi Arabia
   (5) South Yemen

3. According to the map, which Middle Eastern country has to import most of its oil?

   (1) Bahrain
   (2) Kuwait
   (3) Jordan
   (4) Qatar
   (5) Syria

4. Which Middle Eastern country probably has the *most* control over OPEC oil prices?

   (1) Bahrain
   (2) Iran
   (3) Iraq
   (4) Saudi Arabia
   (5) United Arab Emirates

GO ON TO THE NEXT PAGE.

5. Iran and Iraq, although engaged in a religious war, met to discuss setting oil export prices. It can be deduced that

   (1) their economies are dependent on oil
   (2) peace talks were successful
   (3) they wanted foreign aid
   (4) religious differences are unimportant to them
   (5) they will never fight again

6. Oil is most often shipped by large ocean-going tankers. Which of the following would be the *most* logical sea route for Middle Eastern oil?

   (1) through the Caspian Sea
   (2) through the Persian Gulf and Gulf of Oman
   (3) through the Mediterranean Sea
   (4) through the Red Sea
   (5) through the Gulf of Aden

   Check your answers to the GED Mini-Test on page 20.

Answers and Explanations

Practice   *pp. 16–17*

1. **Answer:** (2)   Find the legend code for dust allergies. Check each choice against the code. Birmingham, Alabama, has the highest level of dust pollution in the code.

2. **Answer:** (3)   Find the legend code for oil spills. Check each choice for the largest number and size of spills.

3. **Answer:** (3)   Find the legend code for chemical fertilizer use. Make the comparisons.

4. **Answer:** (4)   The United States has the most pollution. According to the hypothesis, it would be the most economically developed.

5. **Answer:** (2)   The paragraph states that scientists do not know if the "greenhouse effect" is a unique or repeated phenomenon. All other conclusions are supported in the paragraph.

6. **Answer:** (1)   Conservationists and atmospheric scientists share the same concerns. The groups in choices (2) and (5) might not share the same concerns; the groups in choice (4) do not share the same concerns; the groups in choice (3) would encourage deforestation.

7. **Answer:** (5)   Switzerland is the only country without a coast. It would be the most unlikely to have a navy.

8. **Answer:** (3)   Flooding is a major concern of coastal plains. The Netherlands has been invaded, choice (1), but this is an infrequent occurrence. All other choices are false from general knowledge.

9. **Answer:** (2)   Only Italy has both natural boundaries ringing its territory.

1. **Answer:** (4)   Given the area that Saudi Arabia encompasses plus the information that it has a mega-surplus of oil, it can be deduced that it leads the Arab nations in exporting oil.

2. **Answer:** (5)   South Yemen is the only Middle Eastern country listed that has no oil and, consequently, no oil export economy. The remaining countries, choices (1) to (4), are all oil export economies.

3. **Answer:** (3)   Jordan is listed as having a deficit (shortage) of oil. All the other nations are either minor exporters, choices (2), (4) and (5), or major exporters, choice (1).

4. **Answer:** (4)   Saudi Arabia exports the most oil and could speed up or slow down exports to create an oil glut or deficit, affecting prices. Should the remaining countries, choices (1), (2), (3) and (5), come to significant agreements among themselves, they would still not have enough exports to control OPEC oil prices.

5. **Answer:** (1)   Oil is the major export of each country. The war continues so choices (2) and (4) are incorrect. Choice (3) has no relevance, and there is no way of predicting choice (5).

6. **Answer:** (2)   Through the Persian Gulf and Gulf of Oman. Most of the Middle Eastern oil exporting countries are clustered on this waterway, including Saudi Arabia, United Arab Emirates, Iran, Iraq and Kuwait. Of the major oil exporting countries, the Caspian Sea, choice (1), only borders Iran. After going from the Persian Gulf through the Gulf of Oman, oil tankers would go through the Gulf of Aden, choice (5), into the Red Sea, choice (4), and then to the Mediterranean Sea, choice (3).

Earth's Regions II

Geographers do not communicate all their ideas through maps. They may write articles about topics of interest to them, such as population, climate or language patterns. They focus their studies on a particular **region.**

Regions usually studied by geographers are the Americas (North, Central and South); northwest Europe; the U.S.S.R. and eastern Europe; the Middle East; the Far East; Africa; and the Pacific.

Read the following passage about the Far East region.

The Far East region of the world includes the countries of Mongolia, China, Korea, Macao, Japan and Taiwan. These countries have mostly been populated by the Mongoloid race. However, the aborigines of Japan, called the Ainu, are Caucasoid; about 15,000 of the Ainu still live on the northernmost island of Japan, Hokkaido. The climate in the Far East ranges from extremely cold winters in northeastern China and northern Japan and Korea to subtropical summers in southeastern China and Kyushu, the southernmost island of Japan. Much of Mongolia is desert, and Japan, a range of volcanic islands, has little farmable land. However, other countries of the Far East were primarily agricultural until 30 years ago. The chief crop in the area continues to be rice, a food staple in the region. Recently great mineral resources have been discovered in North Korea and China while Japan has developed into a major industrial power. A potential problem in this region is the rapid increase in population, which outstrips the increase in food production. Politically, China and North Korea are communist countries while South Korea and Japan are classified as democracies. Even though these countries are grouped as a region, there are many differences between them.

Spear fishing on the Li River in southwestern China.

Summarize Ideas

This skill involves identifying the main idea and topic sentence.

A **summary** is a short statement of the main idea. The **main idea,** or most important point of a paragraph or passage, is often stated in one sentence called the **topic sentence.** The **supporting details** are sentences that help explain or support the main idea. When reading for the main idea it is helpful to remember these three things:

1. *Examine the first and the last sentences in a paragraph carefully.* Often one of them contains the main idea.
2. *Read the details.* Do they support the topic sentence?
3. *State the main idea in your own words.* Imagine you are telling a friend about the passage you just read. Summarize the main idea in one or two sentences.

Examples

DIRECTIONS: Use the information on this and the preceding page to choose the one best answer for each item below.

1. Which of the following states a need the nations of the Far East *must* address?

   (1) developing more productive strains of rice
   (2) establishing medical training programs
   (3) establishing university exchange programs
   (4) designing better irrigation systems
   (5) implementing a rapid transport network

Answer: (1)   Lines 15–17 state that a potential problem is the rapid increase in population that is not matched by growth in food production. Choices (2), (3), (4) and (5) are all legitimate needs of any nation, but are not imperative needs.

2. Which of the following conclusions is *best* supported by the passage? The Far East is

   (1) losing population rapidly
   (2) a major industrial power
   (3) politically united
   (4) diverse in climate, race and geography
   (5) accepting many immigrants from other countries

Answer: (4)   The first and last sentences of the passage summarize it. Choice (2) is incorrect. The passage states that Japan has become a major industrial power, not the total Far East region. Choices (1), (3) and (5) are incorrect.

Practice

HINT ▷ Try to give a title to each passage. If you can supply an accurate title that sums up the most important point, you have summarized the main idea.

DIRECTIONS: Choose the one best answer for each item below.

Items 1–4 refer to the following passage.

The Soviet population has undergone many changes since World War II. The birthrate has dropped from 31 births per thousand people in 1940 to 17 births per thousand people in 1970.

In the 1980s and 1990s as much as 20% of the population are expected to be 55 and older. As the older population leaves the work force, there will not be enough younger workers to replace them. Another change has been the rapid increase in urbanization. Less than 20% of the Soviet population lived in cities in 1920; now more than 80% do. Consequently, few people are available to work on communal farms.

Furthermore, the Soviet population is distributed unevenly. Many people live between the western border and Lake Baikal. In this triangle are the largest cities, most of the industry, and most of the fertile land. On the other hand, very few people live in Siberia, the Soviet far east, or Kazakhstan. Despite government incentives ranging from increased wages to the opportunity to buy cars or motorcycles, people refuse to move to the new cities built in these areas. Consequently, the Soviet government depends on organized recruitment and resettlement programs to populate these isolated regions. The government is particularly concerned with populating the border along China because it considers the Chinese a political and military threat. However, the Soviet government is finding it difficult to control and direct the changes in its population.

1. A major problem for the Soviet economy is that

   (1) people refuse to live in Siberia
   (2) the work force is aging
   (3) people refuse to work
   (4) too many children who cannot work are being born
   (5) cheap Chinese products are imported

2. Why do people not want to live in Siberia, Kazakhstan and the Soviet far east?

   (1) The climate is freezing.
   (2) They are stubborn.
   (3) They do not like to get higher wages.
   (4) Few other people live in those isolated regions.
   (5) They are afraid of the Chinese.

GO ON TO THE NEXT PAGE.

3. The effect of the rapid increase in urbanization could *best* be counteracted by

(1) building more cities
(2) more productive agricultural methods
(3) more industrial expansion
(4) more army recruitment
(5) increasing the birth rate

4. Which is the *best* summary statement?

(1) Many Soviet people refuse to live in underpopulated areas.
(2) The Soviet government is happy with its population distribution.
(3) The Soviet population is changing in ways the government cannot control.
(4) Soviet resettlement is a success.
(5) Many changes have occurred in the population since World War II.

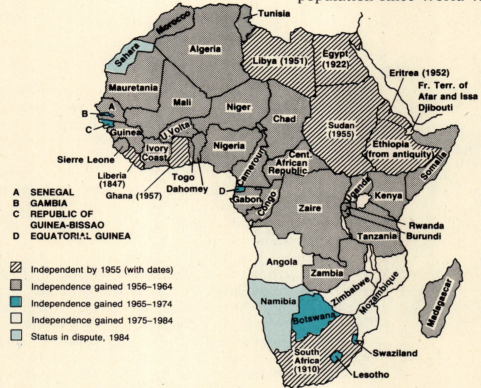

A SENEGAL
B GAMBIA
C REPUBLIC OF GUINEA-BISSAO
D EQUATORIAL GUINEA

▨ Independent by 1955 (with dates)
▦ Independence gained 1956–1964
▩ Independence gained 1965–1974
☐ Independence gained 1975–1984
▤ Status in dispute, 1984

AFRICAN COLONIES BECOME INDEPENDENT COUNTRIES

Items 5–8 refer to the above map of Africa.

5. By which date was the majority of North Africa independent?

(1) 1910
(2) 1950
(3) 1964
(4) 1974
(5) 1984

6. Which of the following countries has been self-governing for the longest time?

(1) Egypt
(2) Liberia
(3) Libya
(4) South Africa
(5) Zaire

7. What country was never colonized?

(1) South Africa
(2) Algeria
(3) Upper Volta
(4) Ethiopia
(5) Tanzania

8. The map of Africa as used in this section is a

(1) special purpose map
(2) political map
(3) topological map
(4) physical map
(5) contour map

Before you take the GED Mini-Test, check your answers on page 26.

GED Mini-Test

2

TIP

Set your own test goals. Try to predict how you will do; that is, what score you will get. Setting a goal helps you achieve satisfaction and builds your confidence in test taking.

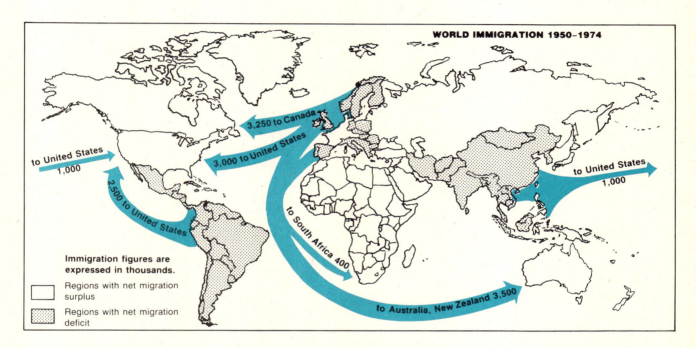

WORLD IMMIGRATION 1950–1974

3,250 to Canada

to United States 1,000

3,000 to United States

to United States 1,000

2,500 to United States

to South Africa 400

to Australia, New Zealand 3,500

Immigration figures are expressed in thousands.

☐ Regions with net migration surplus

▨ Regions with net migration deficit

DIRECTIONS: Choose the one best answer for each item below.

Items 1–6 pertain to the above map of world immigration.

1. In the 1960s South America replaced Europe as the principal source of immigration to the United States. What *most* accounts for this fact?

   (1) growing political unrest in South America
   (2) common language between the countries
   (3) farming opportunities in the midwest
   (4) educational opportunities in North America
   (5) industrial opportunities in major U.S. cities

2. What would you conclude from a comparison between the Far East and Australia?

   (1) Many Orientals immigrate to Australia.
   (2) Many Australians immigrate to the Far East.
   (3) The Far East and Australia receive equal numbers of immigrants.
   (4) Australia has very few immigrants.
   (5) More people immigrate to Australia than to the Far East.

3. The legend words "net migration surplus" mean

   (1) the country is losing population
   (2) more people leave the country than enter
   (3) the birth rate is rising rapidly
   (4) more people move into the country than move out of the country
   (5) the economy is improving

4. Which country has the *least* number of immigrants?

   (1) Australia
   (2) Canada
   (3) South Africa
   (4) Union of Soviet Socialist Republics
   (5) United States

GO ON TO THE NEXT PAGE.

5. Which country had the *greatest* number of immigrants?

    (1) Australia
    (2) Canada
    (3) South Africa
    (4) Union of Soviet Socialist Republics
    (5) United States

6. Which area of the world is becoming a major new source of immigration to the United States?

    (1) Africa
    (2) Asia
    (3) Australia
    (4) Canada
    (5) Middle East

Check your answers to the GED Mini-Test on page 27.

Answers and Explanations

Practice   *pp. 23–24*

1. Answer: (2)   Choice (1) is not an *economic* problem. Choices (3) and (5) are not supported by the paragraph. Choice (4) is false; too few children are being born.

2. Answer: (4)   The last paragraph implies that the population wants to stay in the region with cities and industrial and agricultural resources, not in unpopulated areas. Choices (1) and (2) are not supported by the paragraph. Choice (3) is not supported by general knowledge. People usually want to be paid more.

3. Answer: (2)   The *effect* of urbanization is lack of people to work on the farms. More productive agricultural methods would insure being able to feed the large populations in the cities. Choices (1) and (3) would encourage more urbanization. Choices (4) and (5) are irrelevant.

4. Answer: (5)   This choice brings together all the information in the article. Choice (1) is a detail; choices (2) and (4) are false; choice (3) is only a partial summary.

5. Answer: (3)   With the exception of a few small countries all North Africa was independent by 1964. Many of the countries became independent between 1956 and 1964, so 1964 is the earliest possible date given.

6. Answer: (2)   From the dates and legend you find that Liberia has been self-governing (independent) since 1847; South Africa since 1910; Egypt since 1922; Libya since 1951; and Zaire since after 1956.

7. Answer: (4)   All other countries cited have dates of independence, or, from the legend, became independent after 1955.

8. Answer: (1)   It shows the progress to independence made by African countries. See the Geography Overview, page 13, for a definition of special purpose maps.

1. **Answer:** (1)   General knowledge of current affairs shows that much of South America is in political turmoil. Choice (2) is false. Choices (3), (4) and (5) may have been reasons for a few immigrants, but would not account for the extensive numbers who immigrated.

2. **Answer:** (5)   This choice is supported by information in the legend and arrows. Choices (1) to (4) are false.

3. **Answer:** (4)   This question requires you to put known words into a new context. Surplus means an excess or increase; deficit means a loss. The map discusses migration, or movement of people, so choices (3) and (5) are false by definition.

4. **Answer:** (4)   The Union of Soviet Socialist Republics is not listed on the map as receiving immigrants at all. The other four choices are all listed as having immigrants. You can conclude that the U.S.S.R. has the least number of immigrants among the countries named.

5. **Answer:** (5)   This can be determined by adding the totals indicated by the arrows on the map. Choice (4) has been explained in item **4.** Choices (1), (2) and (3) do not reach the total of U.S. immigration.

6. **Answer:** (2)   Item **1** indicates that South America and Europe are the principal sources of immigration to the U.S. The map clearly shows Asia as another source. In fact, during the 1970s there had been a major wave of immigration from this part of the world. Choices (1), (3), (4) and (5) show no significant immigration to the U.S.

In this section you have learned about the main topics of geography:

1. The physical characteristics of our world
2. How these characteristics influence the cultures of the world
3. How humans affect the physical world around them

You have practiced the skills of map reading through reading and interpreting different types of world maps. Below are more practice items to help you.

DIRECTIONS: Choose the <u>one</u> best answer for each item below.

Items 1–2 refer to the following passage.

Mountains provide natural boundaries that impede the spread of people and their ideas. Consequently, almost all of the world's major cities are found in the lowlands, on the coasts and along rivers.

1. The above statement *best* explains why

   (1) mountains have violent weather
   (2) nomads often travel over mountains
   (3) mountainous regions are over-populated
   (4) people settle along water routes
   (5) Katmandu is located in the mountains

2. The above statement implies that the spread of a society's ideas is encouraged by

   (1) the desire to learn about new things
   (2) the ease of travel
   (3) the military force
   (4) the presence of mountains
   (5) a large population

Items 3–6 refer to the following passage.

Climate in a particular place on the earth is determined by three things: latitude, closeness to the sea and elevation. Latitude, a point of reference that indicates how far south or north of the Equator a country lies, affects climate because the heat of sunrays is strongest at the Equator and weakest at the poles. Closeness to the sea affects climate because the sea helps to regulate land temperatures. Coastal areas are subject to fewer extremes of temperature. Elevation, or height above sea level, affects temperature because the higher an area is, the cooler the climate is.

3. Tropical climates would *most* likely be found

   (1) in mountain regions
   (2) by the poles
   (3) close to the Equator
   (4) in coastal areas
   (5) far from the Equator

4. A person living in a hot climate who wanted a cooler place would probably choose

   (1) the valleys
   (2) a city
   (3) a lake
   (4) the mountains
   (5) a farm

GO ON TO THE NEXT PAGE.

5. A point of latitude can be said to affect the climate by

(1) specifying the areas of the earth
(2) evening out extremes of temperature
(3) establishing height above sea level
(4) increasing rainfall
(5) bringing the land closer to the sun

6. The *best* summary for this passage would be

(1) latitude is the prime determiner of climate
(2) climates are similar at the poles and the Equator
(3) climates are similar coast to coast
(4) islands have extremes of temperatures
(5) climate is determined by many factors

Items 7–10 refer to the following map.

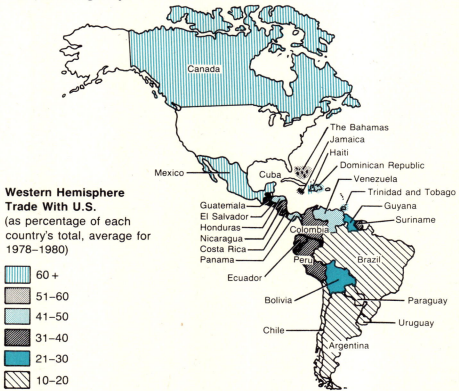

Western Hemisphere Trade With U.S.
(as percentage of each country's total, average for 1978–1980)

- 60 +
- 51–60
- 41–50
- 31–40
- 21–30
- 10–20

7. Which of the following countries has the greatest percentage of its export trade with the United States?

(1) Peru
(2) the Bahamas
(3) Ecuador
(4) Mexico
(5) Venezuela

8. Cuba is not a trading partner of the United States because of

(1) lack of goods to export
(2) political differences
(3) developing nation status
(4) subsistence-level economy
(5) no possible trade route

9. A businessperson planning an export business would probably get the most government support if she lived in

(1) Brazil
(2) Canada
(3) Nicaragua
(4) Peru
(5) Venezuela

10. Which of the following is the *best* inference about Western Hemisphere economies, based on information in the map?

(1) They are closely interwoven.
(2) They are completely independent.
(3) They are primarily agricultural.
(4) They are centrally planned.
(5) Export trade has little influence on them.

GO ON TO THE NEXT PAGE.

Fossil fuels are the world's main source of energy. Deposits are found in all continents, but are not evenly distributed over the globe. At present consumption rates, known oil and gas reserves are expected to last for 30 to 50 years, coal reserves for at least 300 years.

Fossil fuels supplied 90% of world energy needs in 1978 and are expected to supply more than 75% of the needs in the year 2000. The demand for coal has risen steadily since the oil price began its sharp rise in the early 1970s. While coal supplied 18% of world energy needs in 1978, compared with 54% for oil and 18% for natural gas, it is expected to supply nearly 24% of world needs in the year 2000.

11. The passage implies that by the year 2000

(1) use of coal will decrease
(2) oil and gas reserves will run out
(3) more sources of energy other than fossil fuels will be used
(4) more oil and natural gas will be discovered
(5) fossil fuel deposits will be distributed evenly over the earth

12. If oil prices began to drop, you would assume that coal demand would

(1) drop
(2) stay the same
(3) rise rapidly
(4) rise slowly
(5) disappear

13. Demography, the study of human population, is another area of concern for geographers. They are particularly concerned with changes in demography and what these tell about a country or culture. Geographers would *most* likely study statistics about the infant mortality rate to

(1) evaluate adequacy of health care in a nation
(2) add to their general knowledge
(3) define the moral standards of a nation
(4) decide where political borders should be drawn
(5) decide where more hospitals should be built

14. Nomads, like the Bedouins of Arabia and the Kurds of Iran and Iraq, are people who have no fixed residence. They are usually pastoral tribes that follow well-defined routes in search of a food supply for themselves and their livestock. In the last twenty years, most nomads have been prevented from following their seasonal routes. This is *most* probably the result of

(1) nomads joining the industrial workforce
(2) increased political polarization between adjacent countries
(3) decreased food supplies in the Middle East
(4) less available water on the oases of the deserts
(5) higher living standards

15. The Eskimos of Northern Canada and Alaska are often cited as an example of how a physical environment influences a way of daily life. Which of the following is an aspect of Eskimo life which was *not* influenced by the physical environment?

(1) methods of fishing and hunting
(2) development of igloo housing
(3) types of clothing
(4) payments to the Eskimos for federal appropriation of native lands
(5) differentiation of language to the extent of having more than twenty different words for snow

16. The label the 'Rice Bowl of Asia,' which is most equivalent to the 'Breadbasket of America,' means that each is

(1) the name of a sports arena
(2) an agricultural area
(3) a trademark for a popular food
(4) a type of eating utensil used throughout a geographical region
(5) a geographical region that supplies a staple food

Interpret Data

Statistical data is often presented in the form of tables and graphs to make it easier to use and compare. **Tables** use rows and columns to organize and list information in a particular order. Several different kinds of **graphs** are used to compare data visually, show trends and make predictions.

POPULATION: 1950 TO 1980		Increase over preceding census	
CENSUS DATE	Population	Number	Percent
1950	151,325,798	19,161,229	14.5
1960	179,323,175	27,997,377	18.5
1970	203,302,031	23,978,856	13.4
1980	226,545,805	23,243,774	11.4

The **table** above shows the United States population figures from 1950 to 1980. The first column gives the census date. The second column gives the total population figures for each census date. The third and fourth columns show the increase in population from the previous census date in two different ways. The third column shows the *exact* number of the increase. The fourth column shows the *percentage* increase. To read the table, go down the first column and find the date you are interested in. Read the data related to it by moving across the row.

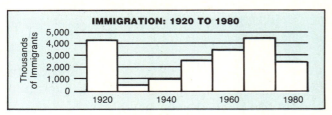

This graph is called a **bar graph** because the data is represented as bars. The bars in bar graphs may run vertically, as is the case above, or horizontally. Bar graphs are not usually used to represent exact data but are used to make quick comparisons. For example, it is easy to see from this graph that the number of immigrants to the United States was highest in 1970 and lowest in 1930.

U.S. POPULATION BY PERCENTAGE OF AGE GROUP, 1984

Age groups: 65 and older 11.8%, 14–35 years old 36.0%, Under 14 20.3%, 35–65 years old 31.9%

The graph above is called a **circle graph**, or **pie graph**. Circle graphs are used to show how a whole is divided into parts. When a circle graph is used to show percentages, the entire circle represents 100%. This circle graph shows the total United States population in 1984 divided into age groups. Each age group is shown as a percentage of the total population. Each sector is the same percentage of the circle as the age group is of the population, making it easy to make quick comparisons.

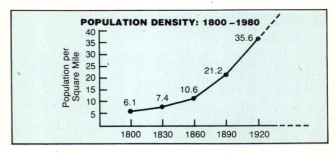

This graph is called a **line graph**. Line graphs are most often used to show changes and trends and to help make predictions. By looking at this graph, it is clear that the population density has increased at a rapid rate from 1800 to 1920. Because of the upward slope of the line, a logical prediction would be that the population density will continue to increase.

Identify an Implication

This skill identifies assumptions, facts or statements that are taken for granted (not proved), and that the author takes for granted.

The data in tables and graphs is neutral; that is, it makes no statement, draws no conclusions and makes no predictions. It is up to the person using the data to determine what it **implies.**

Look at the table on page 31. As you look down the first column you notice that there has always been a population increase. You could conclude, therefore, that the population will probably continue to increase. Now look at the fourth column. The percentage increase in the population has declined since 1960. You might, therefore, make a statement based on this additional data that the population in the United States will continue to increase, but at an ever slower rate.

Now look at the circle graph on page 31. What statement or conclusion could you make using this data? A conclusion might be that the 14–35 age group and the 35–65 age group account for about the same percentage of the total population. By adding the percentages of the 65 and older age group, the 14–35 age group and the 35–65 age group, you could conclude that the over-14 age group is nearly four times larger than the under-14 age group.

Example

DIRECTIONS: Use the information on this and the preceding page to choose the <u>one</u> best answer for the item below.

1. The data presented in the line graph implies that population density in the United States will

   (1) begin to decrease
   (2) continue to increase
   (3) begin to level off
   (4) remain unchanged
   (5) accelerate

Answer: (2) The line has a continual and constant upward slope, indicating that the population density will continue to increase. Choice (1) could have been correct if the line had begun to slope downward. The line is not leveling off, so choices (3) and (4) are both incorrect. Though the population density shows some acceleration between 1950 and 1980, two pieces of data are not enough to justify choice (5).

Practice

As you read, look for implied facts, statements and conclusions. Recognizing implications will help you understand what you are reading.

DIRECTIONS: Choose the one best answer for each item below.

Items 1–4 refer to the following table.

TOTAL U.S. POPULATION, BY AGE: 1960 TO 1984 (in thousands)

YEAR	Total, all ages	Under 5 years	5–13 years	14–17 years	18–21 years	22–24 years	25–34 years	35–44 years	45–54 years	55–64 years	65–74 years	75 years and over
Total:												
1960	180,671	20,341	32,965	11,219	9,555	6,573	22,919	24,221	20,578	15,625	11,053	5,622
1970	205,052	17,166	36,672	15,924	14,719	9,992	25,324	23,150	23,316	18,682	12,493	7,614
1975	215,973	16,121	33,919	17,128	16,674	11,331	31,471	22,831	23,757	20,045	13,917	8,779
1978	222,585	15,735	32,094	16,946	17,406	12,216	34,963	24,437	23,174	21,112	14,995	9,507
1979	225,055	16,063	31,431	16,611	17,505	12,542	36,203	25,176	22,942	21,448	15,338	9,796
1980	227,738	16,454	31,094	16,139	17,533	12,812	37,611	25,877	22,749	21,761	15,655	10,054
1981	230,043	16,917	30,744	15,584	17,446	12,964	39,075	26,509	22,590	21,956	15,923	10,336
1982	232,345	17,279	30,592	15,020	17,304	12,956	39,582	28,190	22,446	22,114	16,209	10,652
1983	234,538	17,616	30,369	14,706	16,911	13,013	40,364	29,462	22,388	22,234	16,504	10,970
1984	236,681	17,816	30,165	14,707	16,384	12,991	41,107	30,718	22,437	22,316	16,746	11,294

1. How many people were in the under-5 age group in 1960?

   (1) 20,341
   (2) 203,410
   (3) 2,034,100
   (4) 20,341,000
   (5) 203,410,000

2. Approximately how many *more* people were over 75 in 1984 than in 1960?

   (1) 500
   (2) 5,000
   (3) 50,000
   (4) 500,000
   (5) 5,000,000

3. Which of the following statements *best* describes what is happening to the median age?

   (1) The median age is increasing.
   (2) The median age is decreasing.
   (3) The median age remains constant.
   (4) The median age refers to the 25–34 age group.
   (5) The median age is the average age.

4. Which of the following age groups nearly doubled in size from 1960 to 1984?

   (1) 5–13
   (2) 14–17
   (3) 22–24
   (4) 35–44
   (5) 55–64

GO ON TO THE NEXT PAGE.

Items 5–8 refer to the following graph.

UNITED STATES BIRTH AND DEATH RATES: 1940–1985

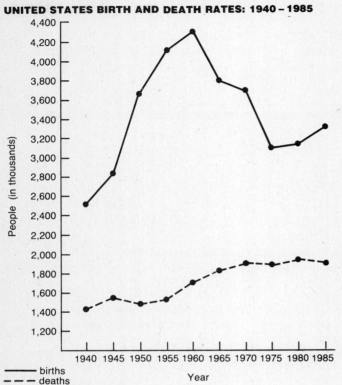

births
deaths

Year

5. According to the graph, in which year did the birth rate peak?

(1) 1955   (2) 1960   (3) 1970
(4) 1975   (5) 1984

6. Which of the following statements does the graph seem to support?

(1) The birth and death rates are about the same.
(2) The death rate is higher than the birth rate.
(3) The death rate increases every time the birth rate increases.
(4) The birth rate increases every time the death rate decreases.
(5) The death rate is much less than the birth rate.

7. Approximately what was the difference between the birth and death rates in 1940?

(1) 1,100   (2) 110,000   (3) 220,000
(4) 1,100,000   (5) 2,200,000

8. Which of the following years mark a five-year decrease in *both* the birth and death rates?

(1) 1945   (2) 1950   (3) 1965
(4) 1970   (5) 1975

Items 9–10 refer to the following cartoon.

The built-in bomb

Copyright 1966. Herblock in the *Washington Post*

9. What symbol is used in the cartoon to depict the urban situation?

(1) buildings
(2) a time bomb
(3) a short fuse
(4) overcrowding
(5) lack of space

10. Which of the following statements *best* states the main idea of the cartoon?

(1) Cities are suffering from overcrowding.
(2) The problem of urban slums is being solved.
(3) Urban areas are bad places to live.
(4) Slums are an explosive urban problem.
(5) Cities are building too many high-rise buildings.

34   **PRACTICE**

Before you take the GED Mini-Test, check your answers on pages 36–37.

GED Mini-Test

③

TIP

Answer all the test questions. Remember that you are not penalized for a wrong answer on the GED test. So if you do not know an answer, *guess*.

DIRECTIONS: Choose the <u>one</u> best answer for each item below.

Items 1–2 refer to the following table.

U.S. RESIDENT POPULATION, BY REGION AND DIVISION, 1950 TO 1984

REGION AND DIVISION	POPULATION (millions)					PERCENT DISTRIBUTION				
	1950	1960	1970	1980	1984	1950	1960	1970	1980	1984
United States	**151.3**	**179.3**	**203.3**	**226.5**	**236.2**	**100.0**	**100.0**	**100.0**	**100.0**	**100.0**
Northeast	39.5	44.7	49.1	49.1	49.7	26.1	24.9	24.1	21.7	21.1
New England	9.3	10.5	11.8	12.3	12.6	6.2	5.9	5.8	5.5	5.3
Middle Atlantic	30.2	34.2	37.2	36.8	37.2	19.9	129.1	18.3	16.2	15.7
Midwest	44.5	51.6	56.6	58.9	59.1	29.4	28.8	27.8	26.0	25.0
East North Central	30.4	36.2	40.3	41.7	41.6	20.1	20.2	19.8	18.4	17.6
West North Central	14.1	15.4	16.3	17.2	17.5	9.3	8.6	8.0	7.6	7.4
South	47.2	55.0	62.8	75.4	80.6	31.2	20.7	30.9	33.3	34.1
South Atlantic	21.2	26.0	30.7	37.0	39.5	14.0	14.5	15.1	16.3	16.7
East South Central	11.5	12.1	12.8	14.7	15.0	7.6	6.7	6. 3	6.5	6.4
West South Central	14.5	17.0	19.3	23.7	26.1	9.6	9.5	9.5	10.5	11.1
West	20.2	28.1	34.8	43.2	46.7	13.3	15.6	17.1	19.1	19.8
Mountain	5.1	6.9	8.3	11.4	12.6	3.4	3.8	4.1	5.0	5.3
Pacific	15.1	21.2	26.5	31.8	34.2	10.0	1.8	13.1	1.0	14.5

Source: U.S. Bureau of the Census, *Census of Population: 1970,* vol. 1; *1980 Census of Population,* vol. 1, chapter A (PC80-1-A); and *Current Population Reports,* series P-25, Nos. 937 and 970.

1. Which region showed the *greatest* percent increase in population from 1950 to 1984?

   (1) Northeast   (4) Pacific
   (2) Midwest   (5) West
   (3) South

Items 3- 4 refer to the following cartoon.

"Help"

from the *Herblock Gallery* (Simon & Schuster 1968)

2. Which of the following statements reflects the information given in the table?

   (1) The population has remained about the same for each region.
   (2) The population has shifted from the South and West to the Northeast.
   (3) The population has shifted from the Northeast and Midwest to the South and West.
   (4) Population size and percent distribution increase and decrease together.
   (5) Change in the percent distribution reflects the country's growing population.

3. According to the cartoon, which of the following is *not* typical of large cities?

   (1) adequate recreational facilities
   (2) pollution
   (3) not enough high-wage industries
   (4) high taxes
   (5) ghetto areas

4. Which of the following *best* states the main idea of the cartoon?

   (1) Cities are great areas in which to live.
   (2) Cities face many crucial problems.
   (3) People are moving back to the cities.
   (4) Cities are solving their problems.
   (5) Bad administration is responsible.

GO ON TO THE NEXT PAGE.

Items 5–6 refer to the following bar graphs.

CHANGES IN FARMING: 1950 TO 1984

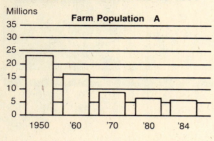

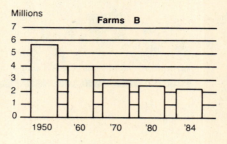

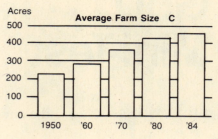

5. Which of the following statements *best* describes what has happened to the farm population from 1950 to 1984?

   (1) The farm population has remained stable over the past three decades.
   (2) The farm population has continued to increase from 1950 to 1984.
   (3) The farm population has declined dramatically from 1950 to 1984.
   (4) The farm population is on the rise after a period of decline.
   (5) Larger farms have meant a larger farm population.

6. Which of the following states a comparison between graph A and graph C?

   (1) Though the farm population has decreased, the size of farms has not.
   (2) The size of farms has decreased as the farm population has increased.
   (3) The farm population and the number of farms have both decreased.
   (4) The number of farms has decreased as the size of farms has increased.
   (5) The farm population and the number of farms have both increased at a constant rate.

Check your answers to the GED Mini-Test on page 37.

Answers and Explanations

Practice   *pp. 33–34*

1. Answer: (4) The figure in the under-5 age group for 1960 is 20,341. However, the figures in the table are given in thousands. Therefore, each figure must be multiplied by 1,000 to get an exact number. Multiplied by 1,000, 20,341 is 20,341,000.

2. Answer: (5) To answer the question you must subtract the 1960 figure from the 1984 figure. Rounding the 1960 figure gives about 6,000. Rounding the 1984 figure gives about 11,000. Subtracting 6,000 from 11,000 gives 5,000. However, you must remember that the figures are given in thousands, so 5,000 must be multiplied by 1,000 to give 5,000,000.

3. Answer: (1) According to the table, the median age is slowly increasing. From 1970 to 1984 it has increased by 3.3 years. Choice (2) states the opposite. Choice (3) is clearly not true since the median age has changed each year. Choices (4) and (5) are not accurate statements.

4. Answer: (3) In 1960 there were about 6,573,000 people in the 22–24 age group. By 1984 that number had nearly doubled to 12,991,000. None of the other choices came near to doubling.

5. Answer: (2)   You must know what "peak" in this context means in order to answer the question correctly. "Peak" means the highest rate. According to the graph, the birth rate was highest in 1960 with about 4,300,000 births.

7. Answer: (4)   In order to answer the question you must subtract the death rate from the birth rate as shown on the graph. Be careful because the numbers on the graph are given in thousands. The birth rate was about 2,550,000 in 1940. The death rate was about 1,450,000 that same year. The difference is 1,100,000.

9. Answer: (2)   It is clear from looking at the cartoon that a time bomb is used to depict the urban situation. Choice (1) represents the city itself. Choice (3) is part of the time bomb. Choices (4) and (5) are not the subject of the cartoon.

6. Answer: (5)   According to the graph, the death rate is much lower than the birth rate in the United States. Choice (1) is obviously not true since the two lines on the graph are separated by a large amount of space. Choice (2) states the opposite of the correct answer. Exceptions can be found for choices (3) and (4), making them also incorrect.

8. Answer: (5)   You must look at the graph carefully to answer this question correctly. Of the choices given, only in 1975 did the birth and death rates both decrease. Both rates went up in 1945, choice (1). The birth rate went up and the death rate went down in 1950, choice (2). In 1965, choice (3), the death rate went up and the birth rate went down. The same thing occurred in 1970, choice (4).

10. Answer: (4)   Since the word "slums" is written on the time bomb, it is implied that slums are an explosive urban problem. Choice (2) states the opposite. Choices (1), (3) and (5) are not the subject of the cartoon and no reference is made to them.

GED Mini-Test   *pp. 35–36*

1. Answer: (5)   The clue to answering this question is recognizing that the percent increase in a population will be found in the percent distribution section of the table. By comparing the 1950 figures with the 1984 figures, it is clear that the Western region has had the largest percent increase in population (6.5% increase). Choices (1) and (2) have shown decreases. Choice (3) has had an increase, but less than the correct choice. Choice (4) is not a region but a division.

3. Answer: (1)   The clue here is the word "not" in the question. According to the cartoon, large cities have inadequate recreational facilities. In other words, it is not typical for large cities to have adequate recreational facilities. Each of the other choices names something the cartoon says *is* typical of large cities.

5. Answer: (3)   Graph A shows how the farm population has changed from 1950 to 1984, and the change has been a dramatic decline. Choices (1), (2) and (4) do not accurately describe what the graph shows. Choice (5) makes an incorrect comparison between graphs A and C.

2. Answer: (3)   By looking at the percent distribution figures, it is clear that the population has shifted from the Northeast and Midwest to the South and West. Choices (1) and (4) are obviously not true. Choice (2) states the opposite of the correct choice. Choice (5) is not a statement that can be borne out by the table.

4. Answer: (2)   The cartoon shows the city crying for help as it is surrounded by its many problems. Choice (1) is obviously incorrect. Choices (3) and (4) state the opposite of what is stated in the cartoon. Choice (5) is not a point made in the cartoon.

6. Answer: (1)   The comparison is between farm population and farm size. Choice (1) states the comparison correctly. Choice (2) states the opposite of the correct answer. Choice (3) states a correct comparison, but it is between graphs A and B. Choice (4) states a correct comparison between graphs B and C. Choice (5) states an incorrect comparison between graphs A and B.

OVERVIEW
History

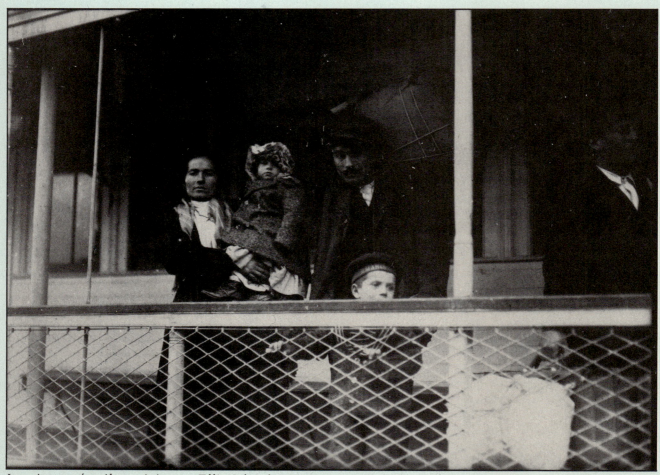

Immigrant family arriving at Ellis Island, 1910.

exploration
travels of discovery
to expand existing
territories

colonization
the establishment of
colonies as extensions
of national interests

The history of America is, to a large extent, interdependent with the history of the other nations of the world. As a country settled merely 350 years ago, our history began as a result of the needs and interests of foreign countries for **exploration** and **colonization.** Our national experience has been the result of the unique contributions of diverse groups of people who have come to America to pursue religious, political and economic freedoms. As you study American history, you will become familiar with the common ideals of democracy that unite Americans from different backgrounds, the challenges to these ideals and the courageous efforts to protect and defend them.

In the first lesson you will learn about spirit of exploration in Europe in the fifteenth and sixteenth centuries that led to the discovery and settlement of the New World. You will learn about the methods, motives and problems of establishing foreign footholds in lands so far from Europe.

In the second lesson you will read how early settlers adapted to the challenges of the new geography of the American wilderness and how their early experiences in self-reliance and self-government helped to shape basic beliefs in American democracy. As you will see, Americans fought and won a revolution—a war for independence—so that the original 13 colonies could become a unified nation.

The third lesson will pursue the problems of a developing nation by examining the great issues and struggles of the Civil War, and the task of rebuilding a divided nation. During that era, **democratic ideals** as to individual and civil liberties were significantly important issues for military, political and social confrontation.

In the fourth lesson you will read further about the factors that contributed to the **industrial revolution** in America: the contributions of new inventions and technology that changed the manufacturing process; the growth of the factory system through the employment of women, children and **immigrants;** and the resulting economic and social conditions that led to the overwhelming need for government intervention and social reforms.

In the last lesson you will learn more about the events of the nineteenth and twentieth centuries at home and abroad that led to the expansion of the United States as a world power. You will see how America's policy of neutrality became increasingly difficult to maintain as foreign domination, totalitarianism and military aggression threatened and offended American beliefs in the principle of democracy for all people. As a consequence of its mission to protect and defend the rights of less-developed countries, the United States became involved in World War I, World War II, the Korean War, the Vietnam War and military actions in Central America and the Middle East. The future of America depends upon its belief in **global interdependence** and its ability to negotiate peacefully with **major powers** of the world to help preserve the basic rights that free people have always cherished: life, liberty and the pursuit of happiness.

democratic ideals
as framed in the Constitution and Bill of Rights, the ideals of democracy refer to protection of the individual against government tyranny; to separation of church and state; to the freedoms of speech, press, religion and civil liberties

industrial revolution
the development of the factory system utilized new inventions and technology to speed up production of goods

immigration
the migration of millions of people to settle in America to pursue freedom

global interdependence
the concept that nations of the world must use their resources cooperatively in order to protect the world environment and maintain world peace

major powers
major world powers include the United States, England, France, Germany, the Soviet Union, Japan and China

4 Colonization of North America

The spirit of exploration in Europe during the 1400s for a faster route to Asia made the discovery of the New World almost inevitable.

The search for the legendary gold and riches of Asia led sailors from Spain and Portugal to sail west across the Atlantic in an effort to find a shorter route to the eastern lands of India and China. One explorer, Christopher Columbus, was certain a westerly route would lead to the rich lands that Marco Polo had described. So it was not surprising that when Columbus sighted land on October 12, 1492, he and his crew thought they had reached India. That he had discovered the New World was not immediately known. The gold that the "Indians" produced was sufficient to convince Columbus that he was not far from the mainland of Asia.

Further explorations convinced European rulers that Columbus' discoveries were worth pursuing. Spanish settlements soon dotted islands and lands of the Caribbean, Central America and North America. The Spanish **conquistadors,** or professional soldiers, were lured by the promise of adventure and riches. Many were also motivated to spread Christianity among the Indians. As one conquistador said, "We came here to serve God, and also to get rich." In the process of attaining these goals the Europeans often forced Native Americans into servitude. In addition, the Native Americans, because they were susceptible to diseases carried by the European colonists, frequently died in great numbers.

As Spanish dominance of the New World grew, the curiosity and envy of other European countries grew as well. France and England began to wonder what the New World might hold in store for them. When they realized that their original goals of finding riches in North America would not be accomplished, both nations settled for more realistic goals. Soon the French and English colonized North America and began to use the land for different purposes. The French, for example, were interested in trading furs; the English, in establishing large settlements for agriculture and religious freedom.

It is in the growth of the English colonies along the eastern coast of North America that the history of the present-day United States took root. As you read about the history of colonization in America, keep in mind the various reasons that motivated European governments to send colonists to America, the effects on the Native Americans and how these lands would be changed.

Use Given Ideas in Another Context

This skill involves taking information you already know and making it work for you in a new situation.

A **concept** is an idea. A **context** is the combination of conditions in which something exists or occurs. As you read about the discovery and colonization of North America, you will be using the strategy of applying concepts from material you have learned (use given ideas) in order to interpret new information in a new situation—a new context.

Suppose you were to read about the Dutch founding of New Amsterdam (now New York City) in 1624. Since you have read the passage on the preceding page, you might wonder whether the Dutch were motivated by a search for religious freedom, a desire for wealth, a hope of spreading Christianity in the New World or the intention of establishing agricultural settlements. By so doing you would have transferred to the Dutch voyages your knowledge of the chief motives for journeying to the New World. You would have applied the *concept* (reasons for the early expeditions) to a new *context* (why the Dutch, also, sailed to the New World).

Examples

DIRECTIONS: Use the information on this and the preceding page to choose the one best answer for each item below.

1. European scholars, for hundreds of years before Columbus, had believed that the world was round. This concept

   (1) was disbelieved by navigators
   (2) led to finding a water route to Asia
   (3) made traveling easier
   (4) led to world unification
   (5) led to safer travel by land

Answer: (2)   The concept that the world was round led to the search for a westerly route across the Atlantic to the east.

2. In a study of death rates among Native Americans following the arrival of Europeans, which of the following causes of death would you expect to rise dramatically?

   (1) starvation
   (2) tuberculosis
   (3) snakebite
   (4) drowning
   (5) poison

Answer: (2)   Because Native Americans had no resistance to European diseases, you would expect the rate of tuberculosis deaths to rise dramatically.

Practice

As you read any historical document, try to determine its significance for the time in which it was written, and see if it has any application for later periods of history.

DIRECTIONS: Choose the <u>one</u> best answer for each item below.

Items 1–2 refer to the following passage.

The Mayflower Compact was drafted and signed on board the ship Mayflower as the Pilgrims approached Cape Cod to found in 1620 what was soon to be one of the first English colonies. It is rightfully regarded as a key document in American history. A part of the Compact follows:

"In the name of God Amen. We . . . the loyal subjects of our dread and sovereign Lord King James . . . having undertaken, for the glory of God, and advancements of the Christian faith and honour of our king and country, a voyage to plant the first colony in the Northern parts of Virginia, do . . . solemnly and mutually covenant and combine ourselves together into a civil body politic for our better ordering, and preservation of our ends, and by this virtue to enact, constitute and frame such just and equal laws, ordinances, Acts, constitutions and offices, from time to time, as shall be thought convenient for the general good of the Colony to which we promise all due submission and obedience."

1. Based on the passage, the Pilgrims were

   (1) deeply religious people
   (2) interested in finding wealth in America
   (3) fearful of going ashore in a new land
   (4) pledged to aid England against Spain
   (5) interested in trade with the Indians

2. In the context of later history, the Mayflower Compact

   (1) helped establish the right to bear arms
   (2) was the basis of religious persecution in America
   (3) was not needed after the events of 1620
   (4) helped establish the principles of self-government
   (5) provided the first treaty with the Indians

GO ON TO THE NEXT PAGE.

Items 3–6 refer to the following passage.

By the mid-1700s the English had founded settlements along the eastern coast of North America. But not all colonies were founded for the same motives. The first settlers in New England came in search of freedom from religious persecution from the Church of England. Maryland was settled by those seeking religious freedom for Catholics, and Pennsylvania by Quakers fleeing religious persecution.

However, many colonies began as **proprietary colonies,** or colonies owned by a proprietor. These English proprietors, given land grants by the English government, sought to use their land grants in America to make a profit in trade and agriculture. Maryland, Georgia and the Carolinas were founded by proprietary groups.

Despite the varying motives for founding and settling the original colonies, the settlers all believed in a representative form of government having its roots deep in English political traditions.

3. In colonial times one would have settled in the Carolinas mainly

   (1) for religious freedom
   (2) to profit from trade
   (3) to avoid paying taxes
   (4) for political freedom
   (5) for fishing rights

4. Despite the variety of motives for colonization, the influence of England can *best* be seen

   (1) in tolerating religious persecution
   (2) in the desire for independence
   (3) in continuing a reliance on self-government
   (4) in trade agreements with other countries
   (5) as a way to expand the Church of England

5. In 1619 delegates from various parts of Virginia met as the House of Burgesses, which was the first representative body in America. This was significant because

   (1) it indicated America was ready to rebel
   (2) Virginia was founded for the purpose of religious freedom
   (3) an important English political tradition was being established
   (4) Virginia was the most successful colony
   (5) Virginia was the home of George Washington

6. "We know our lands have become more valuable. The white people think we do not know their value . . ." is a statement made to officials of Pennsylvania in the 1740s. Who is *most* likely its author?

   (1) a black slave
   (2) an indentured servant
   (3) a prisoner sent to America
   (4) an American Indian
   (5) a Quaker

Before you take the GED Mini-Test, check your answers on pages 45–46.

PRACTICE 43

GED Mini-Test

4 **TIP** A key to passing the GED test is to read for understanding. Reading the test questions *before* reading a passage, map, diagram or cartoon can help you know what you will be reading. They often provide a summary.

DIRECTIONS: Choose the <u>one</u> best answer for each item below.

Items 1–4 refer to the following map.

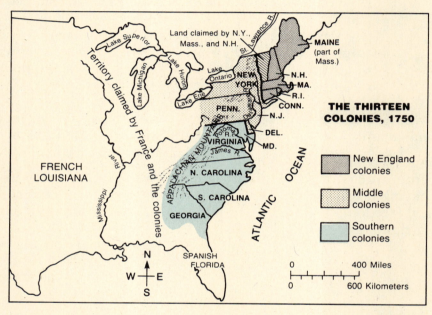

1. According to the map, which colonies made up the New England colonies?

   (1) colonies to the east of the Appalachian Mountains
   (2) colonies closest to Lake Erie and Lake Ontario
   (3) the four northeastern colonies
   (4) colonies west of the St. Lawrence River
   (5) territories claimed by France

2. The largest original colonial land area was part of

   (1) the Southern colonies
   (2) French Louisiana
   (3) Spanish settlements
   (4) the Middle colonies
   (5) the New England colonies

3. From the map you can conclude that

   (1) Florida was part of the original thirteen colonies.
   (2) The original colonies did not extend much past the Appalachian Mountains.
   (3) The coastline of the colonies along the Atlantic was about 800 miles.
   (4) The land that is now Canada was once part of the colonies.
   (5) The Great Lakes provided easy transportation among the colonies.

4. In order to transport goods from New York to Delaware, an important trade route might have been

   (1) the Potomac River
   (2) the James River
   (3) the St. Lawrence River
   (4) the Delaware River
   (5) the Mississippi River

GO ON TO THE NEXT PAGE.

Items 5–6 refer to the following passage.

Colonial government in the 1750s took several forms. Listed below are the three types of colonial governments and brief examples of their fundamental concepts.

(A) **Self-governing colonies**—The colonists directly or indirectly elected the governor and members of both houses of the legislature. Connecticut and Rhode Island were the two self-governing colonies.

(B) **Proprietary colonies**—The proprietor selected the governor and the eligible voters elected the colonial legislature. Delaware and Maryland had proprietary forms of government.

(C) **Royal colonies**—The eight remaining colonies were of this form, where the king selected the governor, and—except for Massachusetts—also appointed the members of the upper house of the colonial legislature. Qualified voters elected the lower house.

5. Applying your knowledge of democratic principles, which statement below describes an aspect of colonial government in the 1750s that was *not* democratic?

(1) Colonists were protected against royal power by separation of governmental powers.
(2) Legal rights of colonists were protected by colonial judges following English common law.
(3) The royal, or proprietary, governor retained the power to veto laws passed by the colonial legislature.
(4) Colonial assemblies could influence the governor by withholding funds.
(5) Colonial assemblies gave consent to enact laws and levy taxes.

6. At the same time, there were many features of colonial government that were democratic in principle and practice. Which statement below *best* expresses a democratic feature of colonial government?

(1) The separation of governmental powers between the royal governor and the colonial assembly provided that neither branch of government could become too powerful.
(2) The colonies supported the official church with government funds.
(3) Voters had to meet certain qualifications pertaining to property ownership.
(4) The governor appointed county agents and local officials.
(5) Laws passed by the colonial legislature could be vetoed by the governor.

Check your answers to the GED Mini-Test on page 46.

Answers and Explanations

Practice   *pp. 42–43*

1. **Answer:** (1)   The Pilgrims undertook their voyage "for the glory of God, and the advancements of the Christian faith" and drafted the Compact "in the name of God." The Compact expressed their agreement to provide aid to each other, not to find wealth, trade with the Indians or aid England against Spain, as choices (2), (4) and (5) suggest. Fear of the new land, choice (3), is not suggested in the Compact.

2. **Answer:** (4)   When you apply your knowledge of later historical events to answering this question, you will find that the Mayflower Compact was the first document to establish the principles of self-government. The Compact did not refer to choice (1) or (5). As you know, the Pilgrims undertook their journey from England to avoid, not to perpetuate, religious persecution, choice (2). The need for the Mayflower Compact was evident as a model for later self-governing agreements after 1620, choice (3).

3. **Answer:** (2) The Carolinas were founded by proprietary groups who sought to use the lands given to them to make profits from agriculture and trade. The Carolinas were not founded as a haven for religious freedom, choice (1), or to avoid taxes, choice (3), or to secure fishing rights, choice (5). The need for political freedom from England was not an issue at that time, choice (4), since land grants were given by the English government to benefit England.

5. **Answer:** (3) A representative body, which indicates self-government, was the continuation of a most significant English tradition in America. Choice (1) makes reference to American independence, which was over 150 years away from 1619. Choices (2), (4) and (5) are irrelevant.

4. **Answer:** (3) As indicated in the last paragraph, although there were various motives for founding the original colonies, the colonists had brought with them from England a belief in a representative form of government. Most colonies were founded on principles of freedom from religious persecution, choices (1) and (5). The passage does not suggest that England either encouraged trade with other countries or independence of the colonies, choices (4) and (2).

6. **Answer:** (4) Since the quotation presents "white people" as something other than the author, it has to be choice (1) or (4). However, black slaves did not possess land, so choice (1) is eliminated. Choices (2), (3) and (5) do not take race into account.

GED Mini-Test   *pp. 44–45*

1. **Answer:** (3) As indicated by the shaded area of the map key, the New England colonies are in the northeastern part of what is now the United States. Choice (1) refers to the Southern colonies, and choice (2) to the Middle colonies. There were no colonies to the west of the St. Lawrence River, choice (4), nor were any of the colonies in the territory claimed by France, choice (5).

3. **Answer:** (2) Using your map reading skills you can see that none of the original colonies extended west past the Appalachian Mountains. Land in neither Florida nor Canada was part of the original colonies, choices (1) and (4). The Great Lakes were too far from the original colonies to provide easy transportation among them, choice (5). Using the mileage key on the map, you can estimate quickly that the coastline of the colonies was greater than 800 miles, choice (3).

5. **Answer:** (3) It was *not* democratic for the royal governor to have the power to veto laws. Choices (1), (2), (4) and (5) are democratic features.

2. **Answer:** (1) The largest colonial land area was that occupied by the Southern colonies (Maryland, Virginia, North and South Carolina and Georgia). They were larger than the areas of the New England colonies, choice (5), and the Middle colonies, choice (4). There were no original colonial lands in French Louisiana, choice (2), or in Spanish Florida, choice (3).

4. **Answer:** (4) Of the two rivers (Delaware and Hudson) in the Middle colonies, the Delaware, which extends between New York and Pennsylvania, would most likely have provided a major trade route. Using the map you can tell that the other rivers mentioned in choices (1), (2), (3) and (5) were in other colonies or territories.

6. **Answer:** (1) Separation of governmental powers is a major hallmark of democracy. Choices (2), (3), (4) and (5) are not democratic principles and practices.

The American Revolution

As Britain's colonial empire in America grew, the British government found it increasingly difficult to maintain control and authority from afar.

The colonists who settled in America found it necessary to adapt to the challenges of their new environment. Owing to the cold climate and non-agricultural lands of the New England colonies as well as the hostile features of the new frontier, colonists learned to become self-reliant. The customs, habits and traditions originally brought from England were, of necessity, modified by the need to utilize the natural resources of the land for survival and trade, to overcome harsh and hostile frontier environments in order to forge new settlements and to establish trade patterns within and outside the colonies to import the goods they needed.

British attempts to maintain control over the colonial empire stirred resentment among the colonists. The colonial spirit of independence became evident in several clashes over British laws that imposed taxes and increasingly limited trade and manufacturing to meet England's purposes. The seeds of growing discontent with what the colonists perceived as unfair restrictions created a wedge that would eventually split the American colonies and the mother country apart.

After many incidents such as the Boston Tea Party and other Intolerable Acts, the colonists decided to fight not for their rights as Englishmen, but for complete freedom from England. Thus, on July 4, 1776, the Second Continental Congress adopted the Declaration of Independence, framed mainly by Thomas Jefferson. The philosophy of government expressed belief that "All men are created equal" and "are endowed by their Creator with certain unalienable rights," including "life, liberty, and the pursuit of happiness."

The War for Independence was hard fought. Finally, it was won. Following the Treaty of Paris in 1783, Britain recognized the thirteen American states as independent. But Americans now faced the new problem of deciding whether they were to remain thirteen independent states, or to become one unified nation.

Distinguish Conclusions from Supporting Statements

This skill involves identifying a correct statement that would justify a conclusion. This skill may involve identifying a main idea and supporting details; fact and opinion; or cause and effect.

A **conclusion** is a reasoned judgment or generalization. It does not repeat the **supporting statements,** information presented in a passage that lead up to a conclusion. It is not the same as a **concluding statement** that comes at the end of a paragraph and describes the result or outcome.

To draw a conclusion, look at the passage as a whole and try to figure out where the author is leading you. As you read about historical events that led up to the American Revolution, think about how an author may lead you to a conclusion foreshadowing the result of several events.

Examples

DIRECTIONS: Use the information on this and the preceding page to choose the <u>one</u> best answer for each item below.

1. Which of the following statements represents a conclusion that may be drawn from the preceding information?

   (1) Land in New England was not suitable for farming.
   (2) The frontier was expanded with little difficulty.
   (3) America proved to be challenging due to its different geography.
   (4) Limited natural resources led to trade for manufactured goods.
   (5) Colonists learned to rely on their own talents and resources.

Answer: (4)   Although colonists were resourceful in coping with the harsh environment in order to survive, they expanded trade to provide goods that they could not produce themselves.

2. Which of the following possible concluding statements is *best* supported in the passage?

   (1) The colonists resented British control.
   (2) Colonial resentment provided movement toward independence.
   (3) British acts limited trade and manufacturing.
   (4) The colonies imported goods they needed.
   (5) Britain welcomed colonial strivings toward independence.

Answer: (2)   Britain's efforts to control the politics and trade of the colonies created growing unrest that resulted in movements toward independence.

Practice

HINT

To determine conclusions that may be drawn from supporting details or statements, look for words such as: for that reason, so, thus, therefore, since, after.

DIRECTIONS: Choose the one best answer for each item below.

Items 1–2 refer to the following passage.

Following the Revolutionary War, the need to form a national government was of paramount importance. The revolution had succeeded in enabling the thirteen American colonies to become thirteen independent states loosely held together by the states that had ratified the Articles of Confederation. Politically, the newly independent states adopted state constitutions that demonstrated belief in representative forms of government and many democratic features, such as freedom of speech, press and religion, trial by jury, and limitations of official power. Economically, America was freed from restrictions on trade, manufacturing and settlements on previously disputed lands. These new freedoms gave free reign to the American spirit of free enterprise and self-government. Free from British rule, these ideas promoted the growth of shipping and manufacturing, and the migration of settlers westward. Additionally, large colonial estates held by royal grants were broken up, and resulted in the increase of small, independent farmers in the South. But these new-found freedoms also brought economic problems, including an enormous financial debt, inflation and the need to interact for trade and political purposes across large territories that lacked good roads and transportation. By 1787 many Americans were ready for the creation of a more perfect union.

1. Which statement *best* describes how the period following the Revolutionary War was an experimental era?

   (1) The colonies were independent states bound only by the Articles of Confederation.
   (2) The independent states adopted their own state constitutions.
   (3) Royal land grants were broken up into small farms.
   (4) Poor transportation in western territories caused political unrest.
   (5) Manufacturers needed new markets for materials and trade.

2. The need to form a national government was primarily due to

   (1) limitations of the Articles of Confederation
   (2) nonworking trade agreements
   (3) disputes over land grants
   (4) the need for freedom of speech
   (5) economic problems within the states

GO ON TO THE NEXT PAGE.

Items 3–6 refer to the following passage.

Revising the Articles of Confederation was necessary for the survival of the new nation. George Washington, Benjamin Franklin, Alexander Hamilton and James Madison were at the Constitutional Convention that met in Philadelphia in 1787.

The delegates agreed generally that the new government must have certain powers to enforce laws, raise taxes and provide for national defense. They also agreed that the form of government should be a republic, in which citizens elect representatives to make and enforce laws, and should have an executive head of government, as well as an independent judiciary and legislature.

However, there were many areas of disagreement. The issue of representation was settled by the Great Compromise, which resulted in the formation of a House of Representatives, where representation would be based on population, and a Senate, where each state was to have equal representation. Southern states wanted slaves to be counted for purposes of representation, but not counted for purposes of taxation. Northern states argued that because slaves were considered property, they should not be counted. The delegates resolved the issue in the Three-Fifths Compromise, which stated that only three-fifths of the slaves of a state would be counted for purposes of both representation and taxation.

The debates and compromises undertaken to form the Constitution were themselves the essence of the democratic process.

3. Which of the following conclusions is supported by the passage above?

   (1) Slavery was abolished by the Three-Fifths Compromise.
   (2) Only the members of the House of Representatives are elected.
   (3) A desire to compromise and accommodate all points of view was evident throughout.
   (4) There was no government before the Constitution.
   (5) The Great Compromise formed the House and the Senate.

4. Which statement *best* explains why the Great Compromise was adopted?

   (1) The tax burden of the Southern states would be reduced.
   (2) Congressional representation from Southern states with large numbers of slaves would be limited.
   (3) Northern states wanted equal representation.
   (4) Slaves would be denied voting rights.
   (5) It settled the issue of representation.

5. The majority of the delegates to the Constitutional Convention were *not* representative of which of the following groups?

   (1) scholars
   (2) farmers
   (3) lawyers
   (4) wealthy merchants
   (5) large landowners

6. Washington, Hamilton, Franklin and Madison were among those known as

   (1) the Anti-Federalists
   (2) the Great Compromise
   (3) the Federalists
   (4) the Confederation
   (5) the Founding Fathers

Before you take the GED Mini-Test, check your answers on pages 52–53.

GED Mini-Test

5 TIP

Remember that map reading is a skill tested on the GED exam. Use the map scale, legend, compass rose and the purpose of the map to help you infer information and draw conclusions.

DIRECTIONS: Choose the <u>one</u> best answer for each item below.

Items 1–4 refer to the following map.

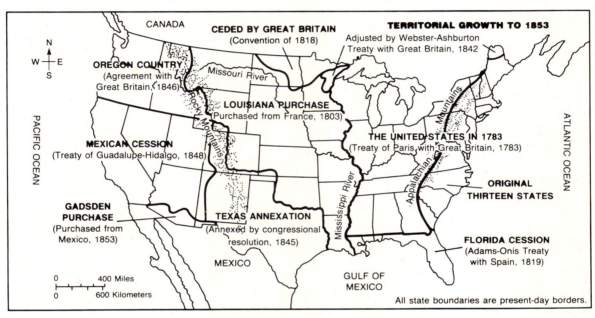

1. To which major geographic boundary had the original thirteen states expanded by 1783?

(1) the Missouri River
(2) the Mississippi River
(3) the Appalachian Mountains
(4) the Rocky Mountains
(5) the Gulf of Mexico

2. Westward expansion was accomplished by many land purchases and treaties with foreign countries. Which land purchase nearly doubled the size of the United States after the late 1700s?

(1) the Annexation of Texas
(2) the Louisiana Purchase
(3) the Treaty of Paris
(4) an agreement with Great Britain
(5) the Mexican Cession

3. From 1846 to 1848, the United States fought a border war with Mexico that resulted in acquiring from Mexico much of the present Southwest and California. This was known as the

(1) Texas Annexation
(2) Louisiana Purchase
(3) Florida Cession
(4) Mexican Cession
(5) Gadsden Purchase

4. The present-day boundary between the state of Washington and British Columbia was created by

(1) the Convention of 1818
(2) a congressional resolution
(3) an agreement with Great Britain
(4) the Louisiana Purchase
(5) the Gadsden Purchase

GO ON TO THE NEXT PAGE.

Items 5–6 refer to the following passage.

Abraham Lincoln stated his senatorial campaign theme in the following passage: "I believe this government cannot endure, permanently half slave and half free. I do not expect the Union to be dissolved; I do not expect the house to fall; but I do expect it will cease to be divided. It will become all one thing, or all the other."

5. Lincoln's reference to the government as "half slave and half free" is based on which of the following?

   (1) the Missouri Compromise
   (2) the Dred Scott Decision
   (3) Harper's Ferry
   (4) Democrats vs. Republicans
   (5) Union vs. Confederacy

6. From the passage it may be concluded that Lincoln

   (1) believed in national unity
   (2) approved Southern secession
   (3) thought the government could not last
   (4) was anti-slavery
   (5) was a presidential hopeful

Check your answers to the GED Mini-Test on page 53.

Answers and Explanations

Practice   *pp. 49–50*

1. **Answer:** (1) The Articles of Confederation provided only a loose and limited structure that prevented the solving of important political and economic problems. Because it did not work, Americans were ready to experiment to form a new government. Choices (2) through (5) are not indicative of the need to create a new government.

2. **Answer:** (1) Limitations of the Articles of Confederation did not permit the solution of many problems that arose after the central government was formed. A new government was needed which would provide regulations covered in choices (2) through (5).

3. **Answer:** (3) The basic tenets held by the delegates as well as the method of debate and compromise throughout the Constitutional Convention showed evidence of their belief in compromise and accommodation. This conclusion is based on material throughout the paragraph. Choice (1) is false; slavery was not abolished at this time. Choice (2), while true, is not a conclusion based on the main idea of the passage. Choice (4) is false; the Articles of Confederation provided a central government following the American Revolution. Choice (5), while true, is stated as a detail in the passage, but does not represent a conclusion supported by the entire passage.

4. **Answer:** (5) The Great Compromise represented a settlement of the issue of how the population of states would be represented in the national legislature. Thus, the House of Representatives would be based on population, and the Senate would give each state equal representation. Choices (1) and (2) refer to a provision of the Three-Fifths Compromise. Choices (3) and (4) are misleading and do not explain the reasons for acceptance of the Great Compromise by all the delegates at the Constitutional Convention.

5. Answer: (2)   The passage suggests the delegates to the Constitutional Convention were among the most prosperous and learned men in America. As such they belonged to well-to-do groups mentioned in choices (1), (3), (4) and (5), but not farmers, choice (2).

6. Answer: (5)   The men mentioned in the passage responsible for the birth of the new Constitution are known as the Founding Fathers. Choices (1) through (4) refer to other concepts or issues in American history.

GED Mini-Test   *pp. 51–52*

1. Answer: (2)   According to the map, the Mississippi River provided the westernmost geographic boundary of the United States by 1783. This new area extended past the Appalachian Mountains, choice (3), but not as far west as the Missouri River, choice (1), or the Rocky Mountains, choice (4). The Gulf of Mexico was not a boundary for this land area at that time, choice (5).

2. Answer: (2)   The purchase of the Louisiana Territory from France in 1803 doubled the size of the United States at that time. Choices (1) and (5) refer to the Texas Annexation and Mexican Cession, which added large territories but did not double the size of the U.S. Choices (3) and (4) do not refer to sizable land purchases.

3. Answer: (4)   According to the map, the Mexican Cession added territory to the southwest, including what is now the state of California. Choice (1) refers to south-western land acquisition but does not include California. Choice (2) added territory from about the northwest to the southeast of the U.S. Choices (3) and (5) refer to territories that are too far southeast or too small in the southwest to be the correct choices.

4. Answer: (3)   Using your map knowledge of North America (U.S. and Canada), the boundary between the state of Washington in the northwest corner of the U.S. and the Canadian province of British Columbia was in the area of Oregon Country, acquired in an agreement with Great Britain. Choices (1), (2), (4) and (5) are, therefore, invalid.

5. Answer: (1)   The Missouri Compromise, which predated Lincoln's senatorial campaign, maintained a balance between slave and free states and territories. The growing conflict between slave and free states was an issue that Lincoln addressed in his campaign speech. Choice (2) refers to a pro-slavery Supreme Court decision that was an *example* of the conflict between free and slave states and the status of slaves in those states. Choice (3) refers to an anti-slavery incident involving abolitionist John Brown. Choice (4) refers to two political parties, not the issue of slavery. Choice (5) was not a factor until after Lincoln's presidential election, when the South seceded from the Union and became the Confederate States of America.

6. Answer: (1)   Lincoln believed that the government (the Union) could not endure the strain of remaining half free and half slave. His belief in national unity is expressed in the theme that a nation must be "all one thing, or all the other." Choices (2), (4) and (5) are not implied and, therefore, cannot be valid conclusions. Choice (3) is false out of context; Lincoln strongly suggested there should be a resolution to the divided condition of the government at that time.

6 The Civil War and Reconstruction

The Civil War divided the nation over issues that affected all aspects of life in the North and South. When the war was over, the task of rebuilding the nation would prove to be difficult.

In the mid-1800s the strain on the ties that bound the nation together became evident. Lincoln's presidential election in 1860 alienated the Southern states. Believing that Lincoln would not represent their interests, and failing to reach compromise on important issues, seven Southern states seceded from the Union and founded the Confederate States of America, electing Jefferson Davis as President of the Confederacy.

At the center of the major issues that divided North and South was the issue of slavery, since it dealt with human beings and democratic ideals. Yet the vast majority of Southerners did not own slaves, nor were most Northerners abolitionists (those who wanted to abolish slavery). Lincoln and his Republicans, though opposed to slavery, did not threaten slavery where it already existed.

In addition to the emotional issues of slavery, the Civil War had other antecedents. For one, economic differences based on agricultural interests in the South and industrial interests in the North led to rivalry over protective tariffs. Additionally, Southerners believed that the federal Union was created by the states, and that any state, therefore, had the right to secede from the Union. The North, however, believed that the Union was created by the people and was indivisible, and, therefore, no state had the right to secede. In Lincoln's view, the Civil War was not so much a war to abolish slavery as to preserve the Union.

The greater resources of the North eventually enabled them to win the war. The term "Reconstruction" refers to the years from 1865 to 1877 when the Southern states were once again established as an integral part of the Union. Lincoln's terms of Reconstruction were based on his belief that the Southern states had never actually seceded, since no state could legally leave the Union. He proposed that acts of rebellion against the federal government be pardoned upon taking an oath of allegiance to the Union, and voters would then be permitted to form a legal state government. Politically, the terms for Reconstruction were generous primarily to regain the South's loyalty to the Union.

However, the issue of providing civil rights for slaves and blacks remained. The Thirteenth Amendment was passed in 1865 to prohibit slavery. In 1866 the Fourteenth Amendment guaranteed former slaves equal protection of the laws. The Fifteenth Amendment, passed in 1870, assured the right to vote.

Recognize Unstated Assumptions

This skill involves identifying facts or statements that an author takes for granted (does not prove).

An **assumption** is something believed without having been formally proved. When we read we assume certain information and act upon those assumptions. But not all assumptions are correct; we must be careful not to assume things unless we have the right information or are aware of our own biases. Remember that an author writes and a reader interprets information based on assumptions that may not be stated in the text.

For example, think how events that happened before the Civil War might be differently interpreted by a Northerner and a Southerner. Think how their interpretations might be influenced by their assumptions of what is "right" or "wrong." What did a Southerner assume following the election of Abraham Lincoln, a Northern Republican? How did later events reflect the assumption that he and his party would not represent the South?

As you read in social studies try to recognize assumptions so you will be reading varied information more critically.

Examples

DIRECTIONS: Use the information on this and the preceding page to choose the one best answer for each item below.

1. Following Lincoln's presidential election, seven Southern states seceded from the Union. This event was based on their assumption that

   (1) the Constitution became invalid
   (2) a Northern Republican would not represent their interests
   (3) Jefferson Davis was a Southerner
   (4) the South was not part of the Union
   (5) Southern states had to rebel

Answer: (2)   Since Lincoln was a Northerner and a Republican who had made his feelings about slavery clear, the South assumed that as president he would not represent their interests in maintaining slavery.

2. Lincoln's terms of Reconstruction for the South assumed that

   (1) the states had a right to secede
   (2) the Confederacy was legitimate
   (3) the Union had won the war
   (4) slavery would be maintained
   (5) secession had not been legal

Answer: (5)   Lincoln believed that the Union was created not by the states but by the people. His terms of Reconstruction were based on his assumption that no state could legally leave the Union.

Practice

DIRECTIONS: Choose the one best answer for each item below.

Items 1–2 refer to the following passage.

The Battle of Gettysburg was one of the most important, yet devastating, battles of the Civil War. It began unexpectedly on July 1, 1863, on the northern side of Gettysburg, Pennsylvania, when a detachment of General Lee's Confederate Army met a division of the Union Army, led by General George Meade. Although an initial Confederate skirmish had run the Union troops out of Gettysburg, Meade managed to establish a strong defensive position on Culp's Hill and Cemetery Ridge. Lee's troops took up a position on Seminary Ridge, which ran parallel to the Union line.

Lee decided on a frontal assault across the open terrain that lay between the two armies. General Meade anticipated the attack. Union troops opened up a barrage of artillery fire against the 15,000 Confederate troops as they marched in lines across the open field. Through heavy fire General Pickett led a valiant attempt to storm the ridge, but Meade's defensive forces repelled them. Nearly all those who got to the ridge were killed or captured. Lee had no choice but to withdraw his defeated army back across the Potomac into Virginia.

The Battle of Gettysburg was over, but it was a costly battle for both sides, with over 6,000 killed and countless wounded or missing. Yet the retreat of Lee's army signalled that the Confederate tide of victory had ebbed. This victory of the Union Army proved to be a turning point in the Civil War.

1. What did the battle at Gettysburg mean for the North?

(1) It marked the beginning of the end of the Confederacy.
(2) Pennsylvania would remain in the Union.
(3) General Lee would remain in Virginia.
(4) General Meade should have pursued Lee into the South.
(5) The Union Army had less losses.

2. "The war is over. The rebels are our countrymen again." You can assume whom of the following said these words?

(1) a Southern plantation owner
(2) a Union general
(3) a slave
(4) a Confederate general
(5) an abolitionist

GO ON TO THE NEXT PAGE.

Items 3–4 refer to the following passage.

During the Civil War, President Lincoln argued that preservation of the Union, not slavery, was the primary issue. He handled the issues of slavery cautiously so as not to alienate the support of border states. However, as the war continued, many Northerners began to favor an end to slavery, and several sources exerted pressure for emancipation. On January 1, 1863, the Emancipation Proclamation was declared. The slaves under Confederate control were set free. The Proclamation also served to confirm the reasons for the war and to gain internal and foreign support for the continued Northern war effort.

3. Pressure for emancipation came from several sources. Which of the following was probably *not* a source of pressure?

   (1) abolitionists
   (2) fugitive slaves
   (3) the Confederate Congress
   (4) radical Republicans in Congress
   (5) European countries

4. The Proclamation had several important outcomes. Which of the following can you assume did *not* happen as a result?

   (1) It inspired the North to continue the war.
   (2) It weakened the Southern war effort.
   (3) It gained support from foreign countries.
   (4) Slave owners surrendered their slaves.
   (5) Equal rights were advanced.

Items 5–6 refer to the following passage.

General Grant of the Union and General Lee of the Confederacy continued to engage in battle until April of 1865. On April 9, facing encirclement and cut off from lines of supply, Lee sent a white flag of truce to arrange for a conference with General Grant. Grant suggested that Lee's retreating and dissolving army should surrender. Lee, after great consideration, asked for terms. Grant suggested and Lee accepted these terms of surrender:

Officers and men paroled . . . arms and materials surrendered . . . officers to keep their side arms, and let all the men who claim to own a horse or mule take the animals home with them to work their little farms.

5. Grant's terms of surrender may *best* be described as

   (1) humiliating
   (2) humane
   (3) ineffective
   (4) courageous
   (5) self-serving

6. You can assume that Lee's reaction to the terms was one of

   (1) outrage
   (2) triumph
   (3) conciliation
   (4) humiliation
   (5) revenge

Before you take the GED Mini-Test,
check your answers on page 60.

PRACTICE   57

TIP

When taking the GED test, manage your time so that you answer *all* the questions. You may want to first answer all the items that are easy for you. Then go back to the more difficult test items.

DIRECTIONS: Choose the one best answer for each item below.

Items 1–6 refer to the following passage.

After the Civil War and Reconstruction, President Hayes followed a "laissez-faire" policy toward race relations in the South. He told black citizens that their rights and interests would be protected if the federal government did not interfere with Southern whites. And indeed, Southern Conservatives adopted a moderate policy toward black citizens. Blacks served as justices of the peace and in the legislature, and were not discriminated against in public places.

However, during the 1890s, conservative shifts in politics strained race relations. Difficult economic conditions, such as the farm depression of 1893, made Southern farmers resentful toward blacks, demanding that they be segregated and denied voting rights.

The Fourteenth and Fifteenth Amendments, which guaranteed black Americans the right to vote, were obstructed by rigid residency requirements that blacks could not meet. They were disenfranchised further by literacy tests and poll taxes (fees paid in order to vote), since many poor blacks were unable to read or pay the tax. Further, Southern legislatures passed laws that established strict social segregation on public transportation and in public facilities.

This new wave of Southern racism resulted in segregation codes known as Jim Crow laws, named after a stage character who created an unfavorable impression of black people. In the Supreme Court case of *Plessy* v. *Ferguson*, the Court ruled that segregation was legal as long as "separate but equal" facilities were provided for blacks. Racial discrimination also found expression in lynch laws and mob rule in the South. Although many blacks chose to remain in the South as sharecroppers, tenant farmers and workers in other skilled trades, thousands of blacks moved west to escape racial segregation. Black leaders such as Booker T. Washington helped blacks by insisting they achieve economic parity through education and trade, while W. E. B. DuBois argued that blacks should protest vigorously against segregation and discrimination.

1. The "laissez-faire" policy proposed by Hayes meant that

   (1) blacks would not be segregated publicly
   (2) Southerners could do what they wished
   (3) the rights of Southern blacks would be upheld
   (4) blacks could not hold public office
   (5) the government would not interfere with Southern white policy

2. Racial discrimination was advanced by all of the following *except*

   (1) *Plessy* v. *Ferguson*
   (2) the Reconstruction Amendments
   (3) literacy tests
   (4) poll taxes
   (5) residency requirements

GO ON TO THE NEXT PAGE.

3. "Separate but equal" meant

   (1) blacks could not ride trains
   (2) racial segregation if equal accommodations were provided
   (3) it was illegal for blacks to attend school
   (4) whites and blacks could not do the same work
   (5) it was legal for blacks to move west

4. "Disenfranchised" refers to

   (1) taking away voting rights
   (2) segregation on public transit
   (3) residency requirements
   (4) occupation requirements
   (5) laissez-faire policies

5. Many blacks stayed in the South

   (1) to avoid segregation
   (2) because black representatives held political offices
   (3) to pursue their occupations
   (4) to foster civil rights
   (5) to enjoy separate but equal rights

6. Booker T. Washington

   (1) favored social and political equality
   (2) opposed the economic development of blacks
   (3) advocated economic success through education and commerce
   (4) advocated demonstrations
   (5) opposed educational reforms

Items 7–8 refer to the following passage.

Earlier, on November 19, 1863, President Lincoln had dedicated a national cemetery at the Gettysburg battlefield. His famous Gettysburg Address linked the Union victory with the principles of democracy, the spirit of a unified nation and the emancipation of people from slavery:

"Four score and seven years ago our fathers brought forth on this continent a new nation, conceived in liberty and dedicated to the proposition that all men are created equal. Now we are engaged in a great civil war, testing whether that nation or any nation so conceived and so dedicated can long endure. We are met on a great battlefield of that war. We have come to dedicate a portion of that field, as a final resting place for those who here gave their lives that that nation might live. It is altogether fitting and proper that we should do this. But, in a larger sense, we cannot dedicate—we cannot consecrate—we cannot hallow—this ground. The brave men, living and dead, who struggled here, have consecrated it, far above our poor power to add or detract. The world will little note, or long remember, what we say here, but it can never forget what they did here. It is for us the living, rather, to be dedicated here to the unfinished work which they who fought here have thus far so nobly advanced. It is rather for us to be here dedicated to the great task remaining before us—that from these honored dead we take increased devotion to that cause for which they gave the last full measure of devotion—that we here highly resolve that these dead shall not have died in vain—that this nation, under God, shall have a new birth of freedom—and that government of the people, by the people, for the people, shall not perish from the earth."

7. In the Gettysburg Address, Lincoln

   (1) emancipated people from slavery
   (2) demonstrated democratic beliefs
   (3) rejected the concept of the Confederacy
   (4) proclaimed Union victory
   (5) urged the Union to win the war

8. Lincoln assumed that his speech

   (1) would consecrate the cemetery
   (2) would soon be forgotten
   (3) would long be remembered
   (4) was of national importance
   (5) represented a new government

Check your answers to the
GED Mini-Test on page 60.

Answers and Explanations

Practice   *pp. 56–57*

1. **Answer:** (1)   The victory of the Union Army at Gettysburg marked the beginning of the end of the Confederacy. Choice (2) does not refer to an issue at that time. Choice (3) cannot be assumed based on the text. Choice (4) is an opinion, not an assumption. Choice (5) is false; both sides suffered nearly equal losses.

2. **Answer:** (2)   Those, like General Grant, who defended the Union believed that the war was an insurrection, and those that fought in the war were rebels. When the war was over, however, these "rebels" were accepted as countrymen. Choices (1) and (4) refer to those who considered themselves to be rebels. Choices (3) and (5) refer to those who did not accept the rebels as countrymen when the war was over.

3. **Answer:** (3)   The Confederate states had seceded and established their own Congress. As such they opposed the idea of freedom for slaves. Choices (1), (2), (4) and (5) refer to groups who were pro-emancipation.

4. **Answer:** (4)   Following the Proclamation, Southern slave owners did not immediately surrender their slaves. The Thirteenth Amendment legally prohibited slavery in the United States. The remaining choices (1), (2), (3) and (5), refer to actual outcomes.

5. **Answer:** (2)   Grant's concern with the parole of Confederate officers and soldiers, and his allowing them to take their animals home to begin farming their land once more, were considered humane.

6. **Answer:** (3)   Lee felt that the terms were generous and he was, therefore, conciliatory (agreeable) to their acceptance.

GED Mini-Test   *pp. 58–59*

1. **Answer:** (5)   "Laissez-faire" is a French term meaning "to let alone." Adopted by the government for the protection of the rights and interests of Southern blacks, it meant a policy of non-interference.

2. **Answer:** (2)   Racial discrimination was evident in all the answer choices except for the 13th, 14th, and 15th Amendments, known as the Reconstruction Amendments, granting basic and equal rights to black citizens.

3. **Answer:** (2)   The case of *Plessy* v. *Ferguson* made segregation legal as long as blacks were given "separate but equal" facilities or accommodations.

4. **Answer:** (1)   The term "disenfranchise" refers to the denial of the right to vote by the adoption of laws that required terms of residency, literacy tests and poll taxes.

5. **Answer:** (3)   Although many blacks moved west to achieve freedom, many other blacks chose to remain in the South to continue in farming, trade or other occupations.

6. **Answer:** (3)   Washington felt that social equality was not possible in the South and instead urged blacks to achieve economic success through education and trade.

7. **Answer:** (2)   Lincoln's assertion that "all men are created equal" and of government of, by and for the people demonstrated his long-standing belief in the ideals of democracy. The speech itself did not emancipate the slaves, choice (1), or reject the concept of the Confederacy, choice (3), nor did it urge war or proclaim victory, choices (4) and (5), since the Civil War was not over.

8. **Answer:** (2)   You can assume that Lincoln did not think his speech was historic when he said "the world will little note, or long remember, what we say here . . .". Based on this, choices (3) and (4) are not correct. He did not feel that his speech alone would consecrate the cemetery, choice (1), nor did his speech represent an idea for a new government, choice (5).

Industrial America

The growth of industry sparked by new inventions and technology brought greater economic independence and national identity to America in the 1800s.

The Industrial Revolution, which began in Great Britain during the eighteenth century, eventually came to America. Following the War of 1812, the British blockade of the Atlantic coast meant that the United States had to produce many of its own (formerly imported) goods. The nation became more self-reliant. Industrial development in the North that began during the Civil War continued to expand with the development of inventions and technology for industry. New industries meant increasing needs for workers, and more efficient machinery resulted in increased production. The economy of the North was additionally helped by the simultaneous expansion of the railroads to the West, which opened new markets for factory-produced goods.

The term "Industrial Revolution" is often used to describe the shift in the national economy from farming and trade to manufacturing. Although the term "revolution" suggests an abrupt change, the growth of industrial America was gradual (*evolutionary*).

New inventions created the technology to replace hand labor with machines, which helped to speed up the production process. Weaving of textiles, once done on looms at home, was now done by the factory system. Textiles were made on machines in a factory by workers responsible for specific parts of the process. Inventions such as Samuel Slater's cotton-spinning machinery, and innovations such as Eli Whitney's introduction of interchangeable parts, coupled with the use of steam engines for power, helped to revolutionize and spread industry in the United States.

As the factory system grew, the need for workers increased. Factory owners looked to immigrants, women and children as cheap sources of labor.

Capital, or money for investment, was also necessary for business and industry to develop. Corporations were formed by groups of individuals for the purpose of raising large sums of money and reducing the risk of financial losses. To raise money, corporations sold shares of stock to stockholders; in turn, stockholders would be paid dividends if the corporation made a business profit. In time, business leaders in railroads, oil, steel and food processing formed large and competitive corporations in order to control prices, production and sales territory; such complete control was called a **monopoly.** Large consolidations and monopolistic practices are now outlawed.

Identify Cause and Effect Relationships

A cause and effect relationship indicates how one thing affects another. A cause is what makes something happen. An effect is what happens as a result.

Events in history are often linked by causal factors. Many factors may combine to **cause** one result. In turn, that **effect,** or consequence, may cause later events to occur. Look for cause and effect patterns. Try to discover the relationship between ideas to better understand *what* happened and *why* it happened.

As you read about the events that surrounded the Industrial Revolution, you will be using the strategy of discovering cause and effect relationships. You may think, for example, about this:

1. What were the factors that led to (*caused*) the Industrial Revolution?
2. What were the results (*effects*) of the Industrial Revolution?

You can then think about the interrelationship of events or factors that contributed to later events happening.

Examples

DIRECTIONS: Use the information on this and the preceding page to choose the one best answer for each item below.

1. What caused the expansion of the Industrial Revolution in the North after the Civil War?

   (1) new markets for manufactured goods
   (2) the War of 1812
   (3) the importation of more products
   (4) decline in immigration
   (5) the development of new machinery

Answer: (5) While the Southern economy was still based on agriculture, the beginning of industrial development in the North continued and was fueled by inventions and technology applied to manufacturing.

2. What effect did new technology have on manufacturing?

   (1) production was speeded up
   (2) production was slowed
   (3) exportation was increased
   (4) the railroads were expanded
   (5) hand labor became more costly

Answer: (1) New technology, in the form of efficient machines such as the steam-driven textile loom, had the effect of speeding up production.

Practice

Identify cause and effect relationships by looking for what made something happen and what happened as a result. Some key words and phrases that indicate cause and effect relationships are: as a result of, therefore, since, due to, in order to, thus and so.

DIRECTIONS: Choose the one best answer for each item below.

Items 1–4 refer to the following passage.

As industry developed in the United States as a result of technological innovations, the need for factory labor increased. This occurrence was based on the availability of vast land in the western frontier that attracted many homesteaders and freemen to acquire land out West, resulting in a loss of labor available for factory work. It became necessary for factory owners to look for sources of labor other than craftsmen, since they were not interested in factory work; a new source was found among young women and children who adapted well to factory work and could be paid low wages.

At first, workers in the textile mills of the northeast were treated and paid well because the company needed to attract additional workers. However, as the factory system spread, factory life worsened as workers faced long hours, hazardous conditions and low pay. The arrival of large numbers of immigrants in the last half of the nineteenth century provided a cheap and plentiful source of labor, and wages dropped further. As a result of low wages, long hours and unhealthy working conditions in the sweatshops of industries, workers began to organize together to correct the sources of their discontent.

1. Which of the following *best* explains the increased need for factory workers?

   (1) the growth of the factory system
   (2) the failure of agriculture in the northeast
   (3) the availability of artisans
   (4) the availability of women and children
   (5) improved wages and working conditions

2. Initially textile workers enjoyed high standards of work conditions and decent wages. What is the *best* explanation for this?

   (1) Companies were responsible for workers' health benefits.
   (2) Workers organized to achieve certain benefits.
   (3) Factory owners wanted to attract more workers.
   (4) Profits were shared with workers.
   (5) Skilled workers were used to decent work conditions.

GO ON TO THE NEXT PAGE.

3. One result of increased immigration to the United States was to provide

(1) more trained artisans for craftshops
(2) a cheap, abundant source of labor
(3) the spread of the factory system
(4) higher pay and better working conditions
(5) increased exportation of goods

4. Labor conditions in factories resulted in

(1) increased production
(2) sweatshops
(3) new waves of immigrants
(4) organization by workers
(5) lower wages

Items 5–6 refer to the following passage.

As working conditions deteriorated, and workers were paid low wages for long hours, dissatisfaction caused workers to band together. Workers came to realize that they would be in a stronger position by uniting as a group to press their demands upon employers. This effort was known as **collective bargaining**, which enabled workers to strike and, thereby, halt production. Labor unions grew out of the need to bargain collectively with powerful employers and corporations. An early union, the Knights of Labor, was an initial attempt in the 1880s to urge adoption of the eight-hour day, the abolition of child labor and the organization of consumer and producer cooperatives. Poor political support and an association with violence caused its decline of power by 1895.

In 1881 the American Federation of Labor was organized by Samuel Gompers to further the economic well-being of its members by building strong unions. There were several reasons for the success of the A. F. of L.: Its membership of skilled workers could strike more successfully than unskilled workers who could easily be replaced; additionally, the organization of workers into separate craft unions with similar economic interests enabled the union to better serve their members' needs than in local chapters. The Homestead Steel Strike in 1892 and the Anthracite Coal Strike in 1902 were examples of early attempts of the A. F. of L. to win wage increases and a shorter working day.

5. Which statement *best* describes why workers formed unions?

(1) to end unemployment
(2) to avoid strikes
(3) a group would be a stronger bargaining force
(4) so production standards would not be lowered
(5) to prevent collectives

6. The effect of collective bargaining was

(1) the formation of the Knights of Labor
(2) the prevention of child labor
(3) to organize workers by craft
(4) to enable workers to halt production through strikes
(5) to gain political support for unions

Before you take the GED Mini-Test, check your answers on pages 66–67.

DIRECTIONS: Choose the one best answer for each item below.

Items 1–2 refer to the following passage.

As a result of rapid industrial growth, people flocked to large cities to find jobs or to be near urban society and culture. Cities served as lucrative markets for nearby farms and as dynamic centers of new industries. Improved transportation, trade, commerce, industry and immigration were all contributing factors to the growth of large urban areas, such as Chicago and New York. However, urban growth also caused problems resulting from overcrowded conditions in tenements that lacked basic necessities for health and cleanliness. As a result, diseases like typhoid ravaged entire neighborhoods.

1. Which of the following is *not* a reason for the growth of large cities?

   (1) increased commerce
   (2) job opportunities
   (3) immigration
   (4) spread of disease
   (5) efficient transportation

2. An effect of the rapid growth of urban areas was

   (1) overcrowded housing
   (2) immigration laws
   (3) better education
   (4) improved health facilities
   (5) job competition

Items 3–6 refer to the following passage.

Rapid industrial change and urban growth left disorder and inequities, especially in large cities. Crowding, disease, illiteracy and industrial malpractices were common. A group of reformers and writers, known as "muckrakers," helped to arouse the American people to demand reforms. Listed below are four major works and themes that led to public awareness and congressional reform.

Literary Works	Themes
The History of the Standard Oil Company (by Ida Tarbell, 1904)	Exposed the ruthless tactics of oil monopolies
The Jungle (by Upton Sinclair, 1906)	Exposed the horrors of the meat-packing industry
The Bitter Cry of Children (by John Spargo, 1906)	Documented the poverty that caused children to go to school hungry
The Shame of the Cities (by Lincoln Steffens, 1904)	Exposed corruption in city government

GO ON TO THE NEXT PAGE.

Each of the following statements describes a cause or an effect of one of the major works and themes described on the preceding page. Choose the work or theme that *most* likely was the cause or the result of the exposure.

3. *The Jungle*, by Upton Sinclair, was written as a result of

    (1) unsanitary conditions in slaughter houses
    (2) unfair labor practices
    (3) poverty among industrial workers
    (4) corruption in politics
    (5) the manufacture of tainted food

4. A work that probably charged politicians with illegal voting practices was

    (1) *The Bitter Cry of Children*
    (2) *The Jungle*
    (3) *The History of the Standard Oil Company*
    (4) *The Shame of the Cities*
    (5) *The Object of Ridicule*

5. One monopoly that was exposed was a result of

    (1) *The Bitter Cry of Children*
    (2) investigations into the Standard Oil Company
    (3) charges against city politicians
    (4) practices in the meatpacking industry
    (5) *The Shame of the Cities*

6. The effect of the muckraker's efforts was to

    (1) provide solutions for society's problems
    (2) inform the public of urgent problems
    (3) reform society
    (4) expand the sale of books and newspapers
    (5) cause riots to protest high prices

Check your answers to the GED Mini-Test on page 67.

Answers and Explanations

Practice *pp. 63–64*

1. **Answer:** (1)   As the factory system expanded, the result was an increased need for labor. Choice (2) was not a predominant industry in the northeast. Choice (3) is not correct since artisans did not want to work in factories. Choice (4) is invalid; the availability of women and children to work in factories is not the reason more factory workers were needed. An increased need for labor was not the result of improved wages and working conditions, choice (5).

2. **Answer:** (3)   Initially factory owners offered workers good wages and work conditions to attract more workers to their factories, since labor was scarce. At that time, companies were not responsible for workers' health benefits, choice (1), and workers had not formed unions to achieve these benefits, choice (2). Profits were not shared, and factories did not employ skilled artisans, choices (4) and (5).

3. **Answer:** (2)   Increased immigration resulted in an abundant supply of people who would work for low wages. Although many trained artisans immigrated to the U.S., choice (1), they were not employed in factories. Choice (3) had little to do with immigration. Immigration lowered wages and did not cause employers to improve working conditions, choice (4). Choice (5) may have been an eventual outcome, but was not a direct result of increased immigration.

4. **Answer:** (4)   Poor working conditions in factories caused workers to organize in unions to demand improvements. Choice (2) describes, but was not the result of, labor conditions in factories. Labor conditions did not cause, or result in, new waves of immigrants, choice (3). Lower wages were part of the conditions that caused workers to deplore their condition; labor conditions did not result in lower wages, choice (5). Increased production, choice (1), had little to do with labor conditions.

5. Answer: (3)   Workers formed unions to build a stronger bargaining force. Unions could not totally eliminate unemployment at that time, choice (1). Unions used strikes to effect better bargaining strength, choice (2). Production standards were not a reason for workers to form unions, choice (4). At the time of unions, collectives were obsolete as a form of worker organization, choice (5).

6. Answer: (4)   Collective bargaining enabled workers to strike and thus halt production. The Knights of Labor was an early effort to achieve collective bargaining, not an effect, choice (1). Collective bargaining did not result in the prevention of child labor; labor acts were enacted to accomplish this, choice (2). Choices (3) and (5) do not refer to the effect of collective bargaining, which was a tool for labor negotiation.

GED Mini-Test *pp. 65–66*

1. Answer: (4)   The growth of large cities was the reason, or cause, for serious overcrowding in tenements, which in turn caused the rapid spread of diseases like typhoid. As the passage states, choices (1), (3) and (5) were all reasons for the growth of cities; choice (2) was a result of growth of trade and industry in cities.

2. Answer: (1)   The rapid growth of cities led to terrible problems in overcrowded housing. Where the influx of workers and immigrants outstripped available housing, the result was the tenements of large inner cities. The passage does not indicate that choices (2) to (5) were effects of rapid urban growth.

3. Answer: (1)   As indicated in the list, *The Jungle* exposed practices within the slaughterhouses and meatpacking industry in Chicago. Choices (2) to (5) are not related to the reasons that *The Jungle* was written.

4. Answer: (4)   As indicated in the list, *The Shame of the Cities* exposed corruption in city government. One type of corruption you may infer concerned the illegal voting practices promoted by city politicians. Choices (1), (2) and (3) refer to books dealing with other themes. Choice (5) is not mentioned and is not a valid choice.

5. Answer: (2)   As indicated in the list, *The History of the Standard Oil Company* caused the tactics of this monopoly to be exposed; that is, the oil monopoly was exposed as a result of this book. Choices (1), (3), (4) and (5) do not refer to a monopoly.

6. Answer: (2)   The efforts of the so-called muckrakers served to inform the public about urgent problems in industry, politics and inner-city poverty. They exposed problems in society, but did not provide solutions or reform society, choices (1) or (3). The muckrakers' books and articles were not written to effect large sales, choice (4), or to cause riots in protest of high prices, choice (5).

The United States as a World Power

After decades of colonial growth and civil strife, the United States was ready to take an increasingly active role in world affairs. By 1900 territorial expansion signified that the United States was becoming a world power.

By the end of the nineteenth century, the United States had fulfilled what President James Polk had termed America's "manifest destiny" to expand its continental growth to the Pacific coast. The first step toward fulfilling its goal of acquiring, in addition, a system of territories governed by the United States, was the purchase of Alaska from Russia in 1867 for just $7.2 million. Though known as "Seward's Folly" at the time, the purchase effectively eliminated French and Russian influence in North America and vastly expanded our territorial holdings. Then, in 1898, during the presidency of William McKinley, the Central Pacific islands of Hawaii were annexed, adding both strength and territory to the United States.

Meanwhile, the sinking of the U.S. battleship *Maine*, allegedly by Spain, fueled anger against Spain, and the U.S. began the Spanish-American War. In the Treaty of Paris in 1898, Spain agreed to give up control of Cuba; additionally, Puerto Rico and Guam—also under Spanish control—were ceded to the United States, and the Philippine Islands were sold to the U.S. for $20 million. During the presidency of Theodore Roosevelt, America negotiated and built the Panama Canal, which extended trade to the Pacific and led to growing political and business interests in Asia.

During the early years of the twentieth century, America under Roosevelt and Woodrow Wilson was concerned with democratic reform not only at home, but for all people. When war began in Europe in 1914, President Wilson initially proclaimed a policy of neutrality. However, old alliances with Britain and France, and hostility toward Germany's goals of domination through militarism, led America to enter the war that involved her Allies and most of the nations of the world.

The Treaty of Versailles with Germany was the result of Allied peace efforts that served to deprive Germany of territory, forced her to make reparation payments to war-torn countries and provided for the establishment of the League of Nations to try to solve further world problems and advance world peace.

Assess Appropriateness of Data to Prove or Disprove Statements

This skill involves applying what you know about fact and opinion, logical fallacies and unstated assumptions, to determine how accurate a given statement is.

Evaluating what you read involves the integration of many reading strategies. Included in evaluation are judgments concerning the accuracy and validity of the information; discriminating between fact and opinion; and identifying the author's unstated assumptions.

Look at some ways to evaluate historical material:

A **fact** is usually defined as something that can be proved.

An **opinion** is usually defined as someone's belief or feeling.

A **logical fallacy** is a false statement based on faulty logic.

An **unstated assumption** is based on something the author takes for granted or implies but does not spell out.

Examples

DIRECTIONS: Use the information on this and the preceding page to choose the <u>one</u> best answer for each item below.

1. Which statement is an opinion?

   (1) "Seward's Folly" was a reference to the acquisition of Alaska.
   (2) The Treaty of Versailles placed an intolerable burden on Germany.
   (3) Wilson kept the U.S. from entering World War I for a short time.
   (4) The efforts of Roosevelt led to construction of the Panama Canal.
   (5) American concern with democratic reform extended beyond its border.

   Answer: (2) It is an opinion that the Treaty of Versailles was harsh.

2. The Treaty of Versailles placed an intolerable burden on Germany. Who would have been *most* likely to make this statement?

   (1) European allied leaders
   (2) the League of Nations
   (3) President Wilson
   (4) Nazi leaders before World War II
   (5) Prime Minister David L. George

   Answer: (4) The terms of the treaty were used by Nazi leaders to remind the German people of their loss of national pride in order to gain support for World War II.

Practice

Evaluate whether a statement is supported by facts, and whether a writer applies his ideas logically.

DIRECTIONS: Choose the <u>one</u> best answer for each item below.

Items 1–4 refer to the following passage.

Following the end of World War I in 1918, Americans looked forward to better times. The 1920s began with finding solutions to economic problems caused by millions of veterans who needed work after returning from the war, and thousands of domestic wartime employees who were cut back from government work. Factories that enjoyed surges of production for wartime needs shut down to retool for peacetime production. Unemployment rose dramatically, and the nation was involved in struggles between factory owners, workers, consumers and farmers, who demanded an end to inflation and recession.

By the time President Warren G. Harding took office in 1921, the problems of the post-war period had been resolved and prosperity was at hand. Under Harding and Calvin Coolidge, the government pursued pro-business policies, while ignoring the unending problems that farmers had with high expenses and low prices for farm products. Between 1921 and 1929, the rest of the nation enjoyed a period of welcome prosperity. Increased industrial production led to high profits and wages as people demanded and bought goods and products as never before. The cultural and material progress of the "Roaring Twenties" changed the patterns of everyday life as people adapted to new music, fads and fashions as well as to new electric appliances, the radio, synthetics and, most of all, the availability of the automobile.

Yet, in the fall of 1929, the bubble of prosperity burst. Speculators who invested in real estate or stocks hoped to make profits by buying at low prices and selling at higher ones. Many stocks were bought **on margin**, meaning that investors paid only part of the selling price. Many investors were encouraged to buy "on margin" from the stock broker. The boom in stock prices continued until some cautious investors began to sell; with fewer buyers, stock prices began to fall, resulting in the further decline of prices. Brokers put out margin calls in an effort to raise money to cover their loans. In turn, this led to desperate selling at any price. The value of stocks crashed, and the nation was plunged into a severe economic depression as fortunes made during the prosperous years vanished almost overnight. Unemployment rose as factories went bankrupt. People lost their jobs, homes and feelings of worth and independence. By 1932 a quarter of the work force was unemployed.

GO ON TO THE NEXT PAGE.

1. From the material in this passage you could conclude that the time period following the end of a war

   (1) heralds a surge in production
   (2) greatly increases the size of the work force
   (3) represents a difficult economic adjustment
   (4) signals factories to close down
   (5) means increased employment

2. Which of the following groups would have prospered *most* under the policies of Harding and Coolidge?

   (1) politicians
   (2) veterans
   (3) farmers
   (4) business people
   (5) bolsheviks

3. You can conclude that the "Roaring Twenties" was

   (1) a period of great social change
   (2) named for the Flappers
   (3) a period of severe unemployment
   (4) named for the sound of the auto
   (5) a result of Coolidge's policies

4. Based on the passage, who benefited most from buying "on margin"?

   (1) speculators only
   (2) stock brokers only
   (3) factory owners
   (4) both investors and stock brokers
   (5) those who owned the most stocks

Items 5–6 refer to the following passage.

When Franklin D. Roosevelt took office in 1933, he promised "a new deal for the American People." The goal of his administration was to pull the nation out of the depths of the worst economic crisis in history. Like that of his progressive predecessors, his aim was to conserve natural resources, regulate business, break down monopolies, save the free enterprise system and improve working conditions. Toward his goals, he formed a "brain trust" of college professors to advise and help him evaluate the government's courses of action. Important New Deal legislation included the Federal Emergency Relief Act to provide grants to states for relief of destitute persons; the Agricultural Adjustment Act and the National Industrial Recovery Act to raise farm prices and institute codes of fair competition; the National Labor Relations Act to guarantee workers the right to collective bargaining; the Social Security Act to protect workers by insurance against unemployment and old age; and the Soil Conservation Act to raise farm prices by instituting soil conservation methods. Additional acts protected consumers, established minimum wages and maximum hours and prohibited most child labor. However, critics saw these reforms as socialistic experiments, citing the New Deal as a break with American traditions of non-interference with free enterprise and competition.

5. Which of the following policies would *most* likely be favored by supporters of the New Deal?

   (1) increased social welfare laws
   (2) creation of bureaucracies
   (3) increase of laissez-faire
   (4) business monopolies
   (5) decrease of government spending

6. Critics condemned the New Deal for

   (1) reducing unemployment
   (2) interfering in people's lives
   (3) protecting free enterprise
   (4) undertaxing large businesses
   (5) limiting federal power

Before you take the GED Mini-Test, check your answers on page 73.

GED Mini-Test

TIP Identifying the main idea and supporting details will help you better understand what you are reading. You will be building your reading skills, a key to passing the GED test.

DIRECTIONS: Which of the terms defined below is the *most* closely related to the following descriptions? Choose the one best answer for each item below.

Items 1–8 refer to the following definitions.

During the 1960s to 1980s in the United States, many new terms became part of our national vocabulary. Listed below are definitions and descriptions of some of these terms.

(1) **Arms race**—Competition between the United States and the Soviet Union beginning in the 1950s to develop nuclear weapons

(2) **New frontier**—President John F. Kennedy's 1960s challenge to fulfill national goals in economic development, civil rights and space

(3) **Civil disobedience**—A form of nonviolent protest against unjust laws or conditions in the 1950s and 1960s

(4) **Watergate**—A political scandal caused by high-level coverups leading to the resignation of President Richard Nixon in 1974

(5) **Reaganomics**—President Ronald Reagan's plan to curb federal spending in order to reduce huge budget deficits

1. The Civil Rights Act and NASA

    (1) Reaganomics
    (2) arms race
    (3) civil disobedience
    (4) Watergate
    (5) new frontier

2. Strategic Arms Limitation Talks (SALT)

    (1) arms race
    (2) Watergate
    (3) new frontier
    (4) Reaganomics
    (5) civil disobedience

3. Concern for discussion at summit meetings between world leaders

    (1) new frontier
    (2) Watergate
    (3) arms race
    (4) civil disobedience
    (5) Reaganomics

4. The involvement of high-level officials and accusations of obstruction of justice

    (1) civil disobedience
    (2) Watergate
    (3) new frontier
    (4) Reaganomics
    (5) arms race

5. Boycotts, marches and sit-ins to protest segregation

    (1) Reaganomics
    (2) arms race
    (3) new frontier
    (4) Watergate
    (5) civil disobedience

6. Legislation to reduce inflation, high interest rates and federal deficits

    (1) arms race
    (2) Watergate
    (3) Reaganomics
    (4) new frontier
    (5) civil disobedience

GO ON TO THE NEXT PAGE.

7. NASA's goal to land astronauts on the moon within five years of the initial concept

   (1) Reaganomics
   (2) arms race
   (3) new frontier
   (4) Watergate
   (5) civil disobedience

8. Sit-ins at lunch counters and bus depots to protest segregation

   (1) arms race
   (2) Reaganomics
   (3) new frontier
   (4) Watergate
   (5) civil disobedience

Check your answers to the GED Mini-Test on page 74.

Answers and Explanations

Practice   pp. 70–71

1. **Answer:** (3)   With the return of veterans, dismissal of wartime government employees and shutdown of factories to retool, the period following a war represents a difficult economic adjustment. Choice (1) is incorrect since many factories involved in war production shut down. Choices (2) and (4) are not representative of the entire postwar period. Choice (5) is not true; employment usually drops for a time.

3. **Answer:** (1)   Choice (2) is incorrect, as the "Flappers" are not mentioned. Choice (3) is also wrong, as it was a period that followed, and was followed by, severe unemployment. Choice (4) is unsupported by the passage. The passage indicates that both Harding and Coolidge favored pro-business policies, making choice (5) incorrect, because it is incomplete.

5. **Answer:** (1)   Supporters of the New Deal favored legislation for social reform considered essential to improve the plight of unemployed workers and their dependents, and farmers who were wiped out by drought and falling farm prices. Choice (2) refers to the large number of government agencies that were set up to administer Roosevelt's recovery acts. Choices (3), (4) and (5) refer to policies that were contrary to legislation passed under the New Deal.

2. **Answer:** (4)   Under Harding and Coolidge, the government enacted many pieces of legislation in favor of business (pro-business). The passage does not indicate that any other groups would have prospered—choices (1), (2) and (3). Bolsheviks, choice (5), refers to a group of radical communists who are anti-business and favor community control of property.

4. **Answer:** (4)   Buying on margin benefited the stock broker by enabling him to attract more buyers by offering to "loan" the balance of money due to purchase the stock. Investors benefited as well by being able to buy more shares of stock for less than the total amount due. In theory, the broker would get the rest of the money due him when the investor sold the stock for a profit. This worked well in practice until stock prices began to decline rapidly, and investors did not have the money to cover their losses—what they owed the broker. This led to further selling and lower stock prices. Thus, choices (1), (2), (3) and (5) do not indicate that buying "on margin" was actually mutually advantageous.

6. **Answer:** (2)   Critics proclaimed that social reform legislation was contrary to the spirit of free enterprise and the work ethic of America by providing economic relief for millions. Choices (1), (3), (4) and (5) were not part of legislation passed during the New Deal.

GED Mini-Test *pp. 72–73*

1. **Answer:** (5)   In 1960 President John F. Kennedy challenged the nation to fulfill the demands of a "new frontier" in areas of economic development, civil rights and space explorations. Thus, choice (5) is most closely related to these issues.

2. **Answer:** (1)   Strategic Arms Limitation Talks have been ongoing since 1972 when U.S. President Nixon and U.S.S.R. Premier Brezhnev first agreed to try to limit offensive weapons systems.

3. **Answer:** (3)   During the 1950s the United States and Russia began to accumulate sophisticated nuclear weapons and technology, and this competition became known as "the arms race." It has been the theme of many summit conferences, including the most recent held in Iceland between President Reagan and Soviet leader Gorbachev.

4. **Answer:** (2)   The break-in at the Democratic National Committee at the Watergate Hotel in Washington was part of a covert effort to hinder the election of Democratic party rivals. Senate investigations eventually revealed cover-ups at the highest levels of politics. For his knowledge and involvement, President Nixon resigned rather than face impeachment procedures.

5. **Answer:** (5)   The Reverend Martin Luther King, Jr., advocated these forms of non-violent protest against unjust laws as the best way to protest segregation.

6. **Answer:** (3)   President Reagan felt that the nation's ills were due to excessive government spending, high taxes, inflation and high interest rates. His economic program, called Reaganomics, called for major cutbacks in federal spending and lower interest rates, in addition to other measures.

7. **Answer:** (3)   Since the concept of having astronauts on the moon arose nearly twenty years before the Reagan presidency, choice (1) is wrong. Choice (2) involves nuclear arms, which were not a part of the goal of landing astronauts on the moon. Choice (4) deals with political scandals during the Nixon presidency, which did not affect the moon program. Choice (5) does not apply to the issue.

8. **Answer:** (5)   Civil disobedience was the chief means by which protesters in the 1950s and 1960s worked to integrate food counters and bus depots. The other choices do not apply.

In this section you have read about significant social, economic and political events that contributed to the course of American history. You have learned about the motives for exploration that led to the discovery of the New World, of the challenges in adapting to and creating colonies in a new land and of the struggle to become an independent and industrial nation. You have read about the problems in defining and defending the ideals of democracy through wars at home and abroad. You have seen that the future of America is based on negotiations to enable future generations of the world to live in peace.

As you continue to study American history, be aware of the cause and effect relationships that major events have to each other. Since history is a study of the sequence of events over time, be aware of the factors that interacted to cause and affect our nation's history.

Remember to use your reading strategies of understanding cause and effect, analysis, interpretation and evaluation as you answer the review questions below.

DIRECTIONS: Choose the one best answer for each item below.

1. One of the advantages of the development of big business for the American economy was

   (1) freedom from government regulations
   (2) elimination of domestic competition
   (3) its influence over government policy
   (4) its ability to exercise consumer control
   (5) its system of mass production

2. One of the abuses of big business may result from

   (1) mass production
   (2) wide distribution of goods
   (3) management efficiency
   (4) control of the labor market
   (5) division of labor

3. Antitrust acts were passed in order to

   (1) favor big business practices
   (2) break up existing monopolies
   (3) modernize production techniques
   (4) limit production and raise prices
   (5) limit the use of non-union labor

4. The Social Security Act of 1935 was the result of efforts to provide which of the following?

   (1) fair labor standards
   (2) compulsory education
   (3) unemployment, disability and old age benefits
   (4) workmen's compensation
   (5) protection of women and children in the work force

GO ON TO THE NEXT PAGE.

Items 5–9 refer to the following Amendments to the Constitution.

First Amendment—Prohibits Congress from interfering with freedom of speech, press and religion, and with the right to assemble peacefully.

Second Amendment—Guarantees the right of the state militia to keep weapons and the rights of citizens to bear arms.

Fourth Amendment—Prohibits unreasonable search and seizure of persons and property.

Fifth Amendment—Provides that a person accused of a crime shall be entitled to a fair trial by a jury of peers and that a person shall not be compelled to testify against himself or herself.

Fourteenth Amendment—Provides that no state shall make any law abridging the privileges of citizens and that no state shall deny any person the equal protection of the laws.

Fifteenth Amendment—Provides that no citizen shall be denied the right to vote on account of race, color or previous condition of servitude.

Nineteenth Amendment—Provides that the right to vote shall not be denied or abridged on account of sex.

5. Which amendment has been the basis of controversies regarding Federal Aid to religious schools?

   (1) first
   (2) third
   (3) fourth
   (4) fifth
   (5) fourteenth

6. A suspect is stopped, is searched and his property is taken from him. This action may be in violation of which amendment?

   (1) first
   (2) fourth
   (3) fifth
   (4) fourteenth
   (5) fifteenth

7. The amendment that provides that no person shall be compelled in any criminal case to testify against himself protects against

   (1) cruel and unusual punishment
   (2) self-incrimination
   (3) double jeopardy
   (4) due process of law
   (5) clear and present danger

8. Which amendment extended the right to vote to a large part of the population after the Civil War?

   (1) fourth
   (2) fifth
   (3) fourteenth
   (4) fifteenth
   (5) nineteenth

9. Which amendment was passed due to the efforts of suffragettes in recognition of their services during World War I?

   (1) fourth
   (2) fifth
   (3) fourteenth
   (4) fifteenth
   (5) nineteenth

GO ON TO THE NEXT PAGE.

Items 10–13 refer to the following passage.

The New Deal years saw Americans busily solving the problems of the Great Depression, and the political turmoil in Germany seemed far removed from efforts to return to normalcy. However, by the mid-1930s, the rise of totalitarianism in Italy, Germany and Japan ended United States isolation from world affairs. The U.S. became involved in World War II following the Japanese attack on American naval vessels in Pearl Harbor, and our declaration of war was followed by a declaration of war against the United States by Germany and Italy. The major powers of the Allies were the United States, Great Britain, France and the Soviet Union. The Axis powers included Germany, Italy, Japan and four other nations. The war involved every country in Europe for nearly four years at a tremendous cost of lives. Finally, Nazi Germany was defeated, and following atomic bomb attacks on Hiroshima and Nagasaki, Japan surrendered, thus ending World War II in 1945.

Steps toward world peace were undertaken by the United Nations, an international peace-keeping organization founded in 1945 by representatives of 50 nations. All member nations of the UN are represented in the General Assembly. In the Security Council, only 15 member nations are represented. Five nations, the "great powers"—Britain, China, France, Russia and the United States—are permanent members of the Security Council. Each of these five nations can cast a veto against any resolution brought before the Security Council. (When a measure has been vetoed, its enactment is prevented.) The other ten member nations of the Security Council are elected by the General Assembly to two-year terms, with five nations being elected each year. Since the founding of the UN to the mid-1980s, the United States had exercised the veto nearly 50 times and Russia had cast its veto about 115 times in order to block further action in the Security Council.

By the 1950s Americans enjoyed a period of stability under President Eisenhower, but events of the postwar years in eastern and southern Europe and East Asia contributed to the growing tension between the United States and the Soviet Union, which came to be known as the "Cold War." European concern about Soviet aggression after World War II led to the founding of the North Atlantic Treaty Organization (NATO) under President Truman.

10. The term "Cold War" describes

    (1) American leadership in world affairs
    (2) a policy of total isolationism
    (3) bipartisan foreign policy
    (4) social and economic conditions after World War II in the U.S.
    (5) efforts to contain the spread of communism in the free world

11. The limitations of the United Nations can *best* be seen in which of the following?

    (1) the use of the veto power
    (2) almost universal membership
    (3) the UN military force
    (4) creation of an international forum
    (5) the power of the General Assembly

12. The early New Deal years were primarily concerned with

    (1) totalitarianism in Italy
    (2) a return to normalcy in the U.S.
    (3) the growth of the United Nations
    (4) support for the Axis powers
    (5) the tension between the U.S. and the Soviet Union

13. NATO was founded as a result of

    (1) the Japanese attack on Pearl Harbor
    (2) concern over the Axis powers
    (3) the growth of Nazi Germany
    (4) the founding of the United Nations
    (5) Europe's concern about Soviet aggression

Check your answers to the Review on page 155.

OVERVIEW
Economics

A construction worker on the job.

goods
concrete items that satisfy an economic need or want

services
work that produces something that cannot be touched, or something intangible

capital
money for investment

The science of economics centers on **goods** and **services.** It studies how they are produced, how they are distributed among people and how they are consumed or used up.

Production is the sum of everything that is produced in a society. These things can be goods like food or services like medicine. There are three factors of production: (1) **labor,** the work that goes into making a product; (2) **land,** or places to work and natural resources necessary; and (3) **capital,** money and any produced good that goes into the process of production. Consequently, costs of production include material goods and services.

Distribution covers the differences in people's incomes. It answers the following questions:

1. How much money do you get for your work?
2. How much of your income can you spend for goods and services?
3. For whom are goods produced?

Income is in part determined by earning power, what sort of wage can be demanded for the type of labor or work that you do. However, some income is unearned. For example, a welfare payment from the government and a trust payment from a grandfather's estate are unearned; no work is done in the society in order to gain that income.

Consumption has two parts: (1) amount of economic goods of the society that will be used up (consumed) in production of goods and services; (2) amount of goods and services that will be consumed by individuals or groups in the society.

Three major economic systems exist in the world today: capitalism, communism and socialism. They are characterized by differences in ownership and decision making. **Capitalism,** the economic system favored by the industrialized Western world, has private or corporate ownership of goods and the means of production. Decisions and planning are in private hands. Under **communism,** the economic system of Soviet Russia and the People's Republic of China, the state owns all the means of production and plans the economy. The end result of communism, in theory, is that everyone has everything they need; the individual gives his best to the community and in return receives what he needs for daily living. **Socialism** is close to communism; the state owns all the major means of production and plans the economy for the good of all, but competition is encouraged among small businesses. The state provides certain social services for its citizens, such as socialized medicine.

In the modern world, these economic systems have become confused with political systems. Because communism and socialism depend so much on central planning, they have become associated in people's minds with dictatorships and autocratic governments. Capitalism, which depends on private ownership and free enterprise, is associated with democratic or representative governments.

distribution
how money and products are passed in a society

income
monetary gain from work or other services

capitalism
minimal government control of production

communism
complete government control of production

socialism
government control of large industries

Economic Behavior

Economics is the study of how goods and services are produced and distributed, how prices are established and how and why these factors change. Remembering a few basic principles makes economics easier to understand.

Every country's economy is based on the exchange of products. Products can be:

1. Goods—physical objects, such as food or cars
2. Services—work that someone performs, such as nursing care or computer programming

Products must be paid for, usually in money, but sometimes through a direct exchange of goods or services. When products are paid for by an exchange, the economy is called a **barter economy.** When products are paid for by money, the economy is called a **monetary economy.**

The **GNP,** or **Gross National Product,** is a measure of the economy. The GNP is the value, either in current prices or at a fixed past price, of everything produced and sold over a year. The GNP includes manufactured goods, food that is grown, public services like education and privately performed services like automotive repair: Everything that is exchanged through the economy is included in the GNP.

Prices in the economy are set by:

1. The laws of supply and demand
2. The cost factors of producing the product

For example, making a lipstick might cost $1.00. The lipstick could be sold at a profit for $2.00. However, cost factors such as advertising and fancy packaging could bring the price up to $6.00. If many consumers wanted that brand, they would be willing to pay that much to be in style.

Wages are set by:

1. The value of the work performed
2. How many people will do the work

A job that can be done by very few people will probably pay a high wage. A job that can be done by many people will probably pay a lower wage.

══ Recognize Unstated Assumptions ══

This skill involves identifying facts or statements that an author takes for granted (does not prove).

Remember that an **unstated assumption** is an idea that underlies an author's argument without having been formally proved. The author might not say "I believe this" or "this is true." However, the argument indicates that an idea is believed or is true.

To recognize an unstated assumption, ask yourself:

1. What supports the author's argument?
2. Is the support stated or is it assumed?

For example, if you look at the opening paragraph of the passage on the previous page, the author states that "Remembering a few basic principles makes economics easier to understand." No support is offered for this statement. The author assumes that the economy is governed by some fixed relationships. It is also assumed that if people understand basic economic principles, they will be able to use them to understand changes in the U.S. economy.

Examples

DIRECTIONS: Use the information on this and the preceding page to choose the <u>one</u> best answer for each item below.

1. The statement "Economists must be jacks-of-all-trades; they must understand geography, demographics and politics" assumes that

   (1) economists should be in the circus
   (2) economics influences many disciplines
   (3) economics is influenced by many disciplines
   (4) economics is a political reality
   (5) too many cooks spoil the broth

Answer: (3) The statement argues that every economist must understand other fields like geography and politics. The statement assumes that economics is influenced by those fields.

2. The use of the GNP as a measure of the economy assumes that

   (1) all economic exchanges can be valued
   (2) items are made and sold in the same year
   (3) our economy is a barter economy
   (4) the economy is stagnant
   (5) the economy is growing

Answer: (1) This is correct because the GNP can work as a measure only if a value in money is assigned to each economic exchange, even those that are not paid for in money.

Practice

HINT Be aware of an author's unstated assumptions in material you read. Use details (facts, statements and opinions) that are given *plus* your own common sense to understand an author's unstated point.

DIRECTIONS: Choose the <u>one</u> best answer for each item below.

Items 1–4 refer to the following passage.

Economic growth often looks as if it rewards everyone. An increasing Gross National Product is a measure of success because increased production of goods usually means that salaries go up and consumers buy more. As a corporation produces more, it hires more people. Experienced employees are promoted more quickly. However, many questions go unasked. What happens when the natural resources run out? How may increased production adversely affect the quality of life?

Underdeveloped countries often jump on the bandwagon of growth. They ignore the cost of an expanded economy in terms of the destruction of renewable resources like trees or farmland. Instead they construct manufacturing plants that will allow them to move into an industrial economy. While the developed countries have found that development brings new problems like pollution, the underdeveloped countries often have an attitude of "We will take care of those problems later."

1. The author assumes that unlimited economic growth

    (1) is good for the economy
    (2) has no effect on the economy
    (3) causes new problems
    (4) is unwanted by developing nations
    (5) causes increased unemployment

2. The tone of this passage indicates that it is from a(n)

    (1) textbook on economics
    (2) editorial
    (3) news article
    (4) textbook on foreign relations
    (5) mail-order catalog

3. Which of the following is considered a drawback of economic growth?

    (1) poor labor relations
    (2) increased wages
    (3) ulcers
    (4) disregard of consequences
    (5) lower consumer spending

4. Which of the following is considered a benefit from economic growth?

    (1) poor labor relations
    (2) loss of renewable resources
    (3) more industrial research
    (4) increased consumer spending
    (5) increased pollution

GO ON TO THE NEXT PAGE.

Items 5–8 refer to the following passage.

In a time of expanding economy when more goods are being produced, manufacturers must find more people to buy their goods. They use advertising to promote their products, coupons to make consumers feel they are getting a bargain and rebates to convince consumers they are spending money wisely.

However, when the manufacturer's present market is already buying as much as it can or will, the manufacturer must look for new markets. One way to find a new market is to change the packaging to appeal to a different group of consumers. For instance, in the 1970s more single-person households appeared, so food manufacturers began to package food in single-serving packages. Another way to expand a market is to go overseas, which vastly increases the number of consumers available.

5. A manufacturer would begin a new advertising campaign when

   (1) he had more customers than goods
   (2) he had more goods than customers
   (3) he wanted to limit his market
   (4) he manufactured food packages
   (5) he wants to appeal to old customers

6. A new cost for a manufacturer in an expanding economy could be the cost of

   (1) labor problems
   (2) packaging
   (3) producing the product
   (4) early retirement plans
   (5) finding new markets

7. Information in the article indicates that in an expanding economy

   (1) exports will increase
   (2) imports will increase
   (3) exports will decrease
   (4) imports will decrease
   (5) exports and imports will stay the same

8. The author assumes that the use of advertising to expand markets is

   (1) an economic fact of marketing
   (2) a trick played on consumers
   (3) wasteful and ineffective
   (4) damaging to the economy
   (5) helpful to the economy

Items 9–10 refer to the following passage.

The American economy is generally considered to go through an eight- to ten-year business cycle. This cycle includes four phases: expansion, peak, recession and trough. The business cycle is a dynamic movement: During expansion, business activity is rising until it reaches the peak; during recession, it is falling until it reaches the trough. Although minor fluctuations are always present, the trend is a rise followed by a fall followed by a rise.

9. The *best* description of the American business cycle would be

   (1) positive
   (2) negative
   (3) unchanging
   (4) always changing
   (5) huge

10. If most people were spending more than last year, the economy would *probably* be in a period of

   (1) expansion
   (2) peak
   (3) recession
   (4) trough
   (5) fall

Before you take the GED Mini-Test, check your answers on pages 85–86.

TIP

When you read a long passage:

1. Read the topic sentence in each paragraph.
2. Summarize the main idea.
3. Scan the questions following the article.
4. Read the entire article to answer questions.

DIRECTIONS: Choose the one best answer for each item below.

Items 1–6 refer to the following passage.

All governments work at stabilizing the economy. In socialist and communist countries, the government attempts to stabilize the economy through central planning. Sometimes central planning matches the supply of goods to demand; often central planning is ineffective. The U.S.S.R.'s Five Year Economic Plans are the source of many jokes and funny stories in Russia.

Capitalist governments also try to stabilize the economy. Since they work with free-market economies, in which the market sets its own supply-demand limits, capitalist governments prefer to use monetary and fiscal policies as stabilizing tools instead of central planning.

Monetary policy tries to control the economy by controlling borrowing of money from banks. This regulates money spending. If the government wants to expand the economy, it can lower interest rates. Money becomes more available. People are likely to spend more. When spending and demand go up, production will also go up and the increased GNP (Gross National Product) will make the economy look healthy. Monetary policy also works in reverse. If inflation is rising too rapidly and money is losing value too quickly, the central bank can raise interest rates. Less money is borrowed; people have less money to spend; demand goes down; supply and production decrease. Unfortunately, when production decreases, unemployment will increase, and the government will have another economic problem to manipulate.

Fiscal policy controls demand by regulating government spending. If the government wants to expand the economy, reducing unemployment and increasing consumer spending, it increases government spending. If the government wants to limit the amount of money in circulation because inflation is too rapid, it decreases spending and/or raises taxes. Consequently, the amount of money in circulation is decreased; demand is decreased; and production is decreased. Unfortunately, the specter of unemployment again raises its head.

On paper both monetary and fiscal policy look as if they should work. However, both illustrate the gap between theory and practice. Consumer expectations always increase. People expect to live better than their parents did. People also resist any cutback in government spending that changes their life style. They have no desire to tighten their belts short-term in the long-term interest of the economy.

GO ON TO THE NEXT PAGE.

1. The statement that the U.S.S.R.'s Five Year Economic Plans are the source of jokes and stories implies that

    (1) economics is funny
    (2) economic planning is absurd
    (3) the Soviet plans do not work
    (4) Russians have a good sense of humor
    (5) Soviet economic planning is on target

2. Which of the following is the *best* description of a free-market economy?

    (1) Supply and demand depend on taxes.
    (2) Supply and demand are guaranteed by the Constitution.
    (3) Supply and demand are set in the open market.
    (4) The government controls supply, but not demand.
    (5) The government controls demand, but not supply.

3. In a period of inflation a capitalist government would *most* likely be

    (1) raising interest rates
    (2) firing civil servants
    (3) limiting military spending
    (4) increasing unemployment services
    (5) lending more money

4. If a capitalist government were trying to control runaway inflation, it would *most* likely increase

    (1) defense spending
    (2) interest rates
    (3) unemployment
    (4) demand for services
    (5) money supply

5. The purpose of this article is to define

    (1) stable economies
    (2) central economic planning
    (3) ways in which governments regulate the economy
    (4) problems of monetary policy
    (5) fiscal and monetary policy

6. Which of the following is the *best* summary of the passage?

    (1) Economic theories do not really work.
    (2) Government attempts to stabilize the economy do not succeed completely.
    (3) The future is always better than the past.
    (4) The economy is static and predictable.
    (5) People are only out for themselves, regardless of the public good.

Check your answers to the GED Mini-Test on page 86.

Answers and Explanations

Practice *pp. 82–83*

1. **Answer:** (3)   This is correct from the clue words "often looks as if" and the questions at the end of the first paragraph. Choice (1) is implied; choices (2), (4) and (5) are false from information in the text.

2. **Answer:** (2)   This is correct because the author is trying to make people stop and think. Choices (1), (3) and (4) are wrong because textbooks and news articles are objective; choice (5) is wrong because a catalog sells goods, not ideas.

3. **Answer:** (4)   This is correct from assumptions given in the questions at the end of the first paragraph. Choice (2) is listed as a benefit; choices (1) and (3) are not mentioned; choice (5) is incorrect from information in the first paragraph.

4. **Answer:** (4)   This is correct from the first paragraph. The author considers choices (2) and (5) to be problems caused by growth. Choices (1) and (3) are not mentioned in the text.

5. **Answer:** (2)   This is correct because advertising is defined as a way of getting people to buy more. The manufacturer wants people to buy more when he has more goods than customers. Choice (1) is the opposite; if choice (3) were correct he would not advertise; choice (4) is irrelevant; for choice (5) a *new* advertising campaign is not necessary.

6. **Answer:** (5)   This is correct from the main idea of the text; when more goods are produced, more people must be found to buy. Choices (2) and (3) will always be costs of manufacturing; therefore, they are not new. Choices (1) and (4) would be costs when production was restricted.

7. **Answer:** (1)   This is correct from the information on developing overseas, or export, markets. Choice (2) does not necessarily follow; choices (3) and (4) are more likely in a tightening economy; choice (5) contradicts choice (1).

8. **Answer:** (1)   This is correct because the author accepts marketing products as an economic fact. Choice (2) is not mentioned. Choice (3), although it may be true for some marketing strategies, is not mentioned. Choices (4) and (5) are not pertinent to this passage on marketing.

9. **Answer:** (4)   This is a restatement of the main idea that the business cycle is dynamic. Choice (3) contradicts the main idea; choices (1) and (2) are value judgments; choice (5) has no support.

10. **Answer:** (1)   This involves considering the length of the business cycle and the idea of expansion or growth. If wages and spending go up, either choice (1) or choice (2) must be correct, and the probability is choice (1) because it lasts longer than the peak.

GED Mini-Test   *pp. 84–85*

1. **Answer:** (3)   This is correct because the implication is that the Soviet plans are ineffective, therefore funny. Choices (1), (2) and (4) are distractors. Choice (5) is incorrect because people would not laugh at plans that worked.

2. **Answer:** (3)   This is correct from the statement in apposition to free-market economies.

3. **Answer:** (5)   This is correct because inflation indicates that a lot of money is being spent. Choices (1), (2) and (3) are all ways of limiting money available. Choice (4) would be a response to unemployment, but during inflation unemployment should not be a problem.

4. **Answer:** (2)   To control inflation the government would reduce the money supply and/or spending. Raising interest rates limits money borrowed. Choices (1), (4) and (5) all increase the money supply or spending. Choice (3) is a by-product of government action, not the action itself.

5. **Answer:** (3)   This is correct because it is the best restatement of a summary of the article. Choices (1), (2), (4) and (5) are all topics discussed, but are not as inclusive and complete as choice (3).

6. **Answer:** (2)   This combines all the ideas in the paragraph: different ways of stabilizing the economy and how they do not succeed. Choices (1) and (3) are too general. Choice (5) is a detail. Choice (4) is incorrect.

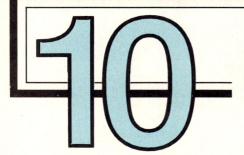

10 Labor and the Economy

In the United States, labor's voice has grown more powerful over the years. Labor's influence on the economy has steadily increased.

Profit, the difference between production cost and price to the consumer, is the goal of corporations in an industrial society. Since wages are a cost of production, corporations' interest is to keep wages low in order to keep profit high. But the wage that is a cost to the corporation is a salary to the worker. It is in the workers' self-interest to keep wages high so that they can buy needed and wanted items for themselves and their families. The catch is that labor's wages equal, in part, management's costs.

Labor has found that one worker has only one voice, and one voice by itself is almost unheard. However, the worker who is a union member has a collective voice that is heard. Why? Labor has a special power over management; labor can choose to work or to **strike,** to refuse to work.

When unions were first established, labor's power was limited by law and by the lack of financial support for striking workers. Now American law recognizes the workers' right to join a union, to organize others and to strike. The **National Labor Relations Act of 1935** requires employers to bargain with a union favored by a majority of the workers and defines certain labor practices as unfair. These unfair and illegal labor practices include firing because of union activity, discrimination against union members in favor of non-union members and interference with employees trying to organize unions or bargain collectively. Many concerned citizens felt that the NLRA was excessively pro-labor. The **Labor Management Relations Act of 1947 (Taft-Hartley Act)** was passed to balance the power of company management and the power of labor; it requires labor to bargain with employers, thus setting the stage for collective bargaining.

Collective bargaining is contract negotiation between management and labor by the union on behalf of all employees. Since the 1930s collective bargaining has increased wages and salaries, health and vacation benefits and company liability for accidents and health hazards. If a union comes to the bargaining table, and management and the union cannot agree on a new contract, the union may choose to strike. Sometimes the threat of a strike causes management to agree to a wage increase. Sometimes the threat must be realized before management raises wages.

Management and labor now communicate successfully. Although they sit on opposite sides of the table, each is skilled at presenting a viewpoint.

Identify Cause and Effect Relationships

A cause and effect relationship indicates how one thing affects another. A cause is what makes something happen. An effect is what happens as a result.

Cause

Why did this happen?

Effect

What were the results?

Social studies examines the causes and the effects of human social behavior. Many articles answer the questions:

1. Why did this happen? or What are the *causes*?
2. What are the results? or What are the *effects* of an event?

Articles based on cause and effect ask you to **analyze,** or break down, an argument. Ask yourself these questions as you read the articles in this lesson. Try to distinguish between causes and effects that are *stated* and those that are *implied*, but not stated.

Examples

DIRECTIONS: Use the information on this and the preceding page to choose the one best answer for each item below.

1. Which is *not* an effect of the conflict between labor and management?

   (1) They sit on opposite sides of the table.
   (2) They place a different monetary value on work.
   (3) Labor has one voice and management has many.
   (4) Management and labor practice collective bargaining.
   (5) Workers have the right to strike.

   Answer: (3)   This choice is the only statement which is false. Labor has unions or a collective voice as does management. Choices (1), (2), (4) and (5) are all true to a greater or lesser degree.

2. What would happen *first* if a city did not want to increase teacher salaries?

   (1) The teachers would strike.
   (2) The city would close the schools.
   (3) The teachers' union would picket the school board building.
   (4) Teachers would take a cut in pay.
   (5) The teachers' union would bargain with the school board.

   Answer: (5)   This is the best choice because the union would negotiate before it would strike, choice (1), picket, choice (3), accept a pay cut, choice (4). Cities try to avoid closing schools, choice (2).

Practice

Remember to ask yourself: Why did this happen? and What were the effects or results? These questions will help you answer cause and effect items.

DIRECTIONS: Choose the one best answer for each item below.

Items 1–4 refer to the following passage.

Income in the United States is distributed unequally. Although the U.S. is considered a middle-class society, the poorest fifth of our country earns only 5% of the income while the richest fifth earns 40% of the income. In 1984, 11% of U.S. adults and 21% of U.S. children were at poverty levels. Many of these poor lack the education necessary to hold a job in our technological society.

The difference in income between the wealthy and the poor has increased over the past decade. Prices for necessities like food and housing have increased more rapidly than the minimum wage. Consequently, the poor have become poorer in terms of their ability to pay for necessities.

1. What explanation for unequal distribution of income does the author offer?

   (1) Cost of food has outstripped cost of housing.
   (2) There is a lack of appropriate schooling.
   (3) People pretend to be middle class.
   (4) Prices have increased more rapidly than wages.
   (5) Many people are at poverty level.

2. Twice as many children as adults are at poverty level. What reason for this can be inferred from the article?

   (1) They are neglected by their parents.
   (2) They do not earn income.
   (3) Supporting a child costs money.
   (4) The poor have more children.
   (5) Children eat too much.

3. According to the author, which of the following is an effect of more rapid increase in cost of necessities than in wages?

   (1) more divergent income distribution
   (2) more equal income distribution
   (3) less money for social welfare programs
   (4) more poor children
   (5) more people in the middle class

4. The *most* probable political effect of unequal income distribution on the poor would be

   (1) growing conservatism
   (2) frustration
   (3) non-voting
   (4) more idealism
   (5) increased activism

GO ON TO THE NEXT PAGE.

Items 5–6 refer to the following cartoon.

"We plan to bargain all night until an agreement is reached."

5. The main idea of the cartoon is

(1) collective bargaining is exhausting
(2) management always lies
(3) labor always lies
(4) the media has a right to know the facts
(5) labor and management agreed to maintain the image of round-the-clock negotiations

6. What is the probable result of the action depicted in the cartoon?

(1) Agreement will be reached.
(2) Negotiations will continue after both parties have rested.
(3) The press spreads more lies to the public.
(4) The negotiators give up and the workers go on strike.
(5) The corporation enters bankruptcy.

7. Recently the union representing airline employees sued a major airline for employees' losses that were caused by the airline firing striking employees. This is an example of

(1) collective bargaining
(2) court review of labor-management practices
(3) strike-breaking
(4) double jeopardy
(5) picketing

8. The union representing longshoremen and dockworkers strikes, closing business at U.S. ports. The strike puts pressure on

(1) consumers
(2) union officials
(3) manufacturers
(4) the government
(5) importers

Before you take the GED Mini-Test, check your answers on pages 92–93.

GED Mini-Test

10

TIP

If taking notes helps you study, take notes when reading a test passage. Writing ideas in your own words makes them easier to understand, especially those that are complicated. Use your notes to help you answer the GED test questions.

DIRECTIONS: Choose the <u>one</u> best answer for each item below.

Items 1–4 refer to the following passage.

Teenage unemployment is a severe problem in the United States economy. Many teenagers choose not to continue their education after high school. Then they find out how difficult it is to get a good-paying or interesting job without further education.

Black female teenagers have reached an unemployment rate of 40% at a time when the average unemployment rate for the United States is 11%. While many of these young women may be married or caring for young children, some have just given up the search for jobs. Working at a fast-food parlor or cleaning office buildings may be an option for a short time, but few teenagers look forward to a lifetime of frying hamburgers or scrubbing toilets. In fact, McDonald's now tries to hire retirees to replace some of the teenagers who are no longer applying for jobs.

Another frightening statistic is the number of teenagers who are not in school and not in the labor force. In 1975 and 1976 the proportion of male teenagers who were neither in school nor working nor looking for work was 32.5%, almost a third of the male teenage population. What will happen to these boys in later years? How will they begin to support themselves? How will they support their families?

More education is still a crucial factor in employment. Better educated people have a better chance of getting and keeping jobs at all levels of the economy. Vocational training that is targeted to future job requirements helps some teenagers find jobs. So do apprenticeship or work-study programs in which the teenager works with a master craftsman. However, personal characteristics like perseverance and determination often make the difference between the person who gets employment and the one who does not.

1. A probable effect of continued teenage unemployment is

    (1) a better-educated public
    (2) more children at poverty level
    (3) more satisfied citizens
    (4) fewer workers in fast-food industries
    (5) increased minimum wage

2. Which government program to increase teenage employment would the author support?

    (1) more government cafeteria jobs
    (2) home-based industries
    (3) more day-care centers
    (4) vocational training
    (5) parenting classes

GO ON TO THE NEXT PAGE.

3. The author implies that the black female teenage unemployment rate is so high because these young women are

(1) uneducated
(2) unhappy
(3) frustrated
(4) too busy
(5) continuing their education

4. The government has no control over which of the following job qualifications?

(1) years of education
(2) type of education
(3) training programs
(4) attitude toward work
(5) number of jobs available

Items 5–6 refer to the following passage.

The International Ladies Garment Workers' Union (ILGWU) is concerned over what they call "sweatshop conditions" in rural Iowa. The union accuses Bordeaux, Inc., of Clarinda, Iowa, of violating the federal regulations that outlaw womenswear being commercially made at home.

The company began manufacturing decorated sweatsuits in 1980, and within six years has sales figures in the three million dollar range. It employs from 100 to 150 women who work at home using their own sewing machines and the company's material. The pay is about $2.45 per piece, or $1.12 if the work does not pass inspection.

Some workers figure they earn from $4.00 to $9.00 an hour and, in this economically depressed farm area, are pleased to have the work. Other workers have complained to the ILGWU that the hourly rate is more like $1.85 (which is illegal under the minimum wage law). They also complained of the lack of overtime pay or any other benefits.

The Labor Department is investigating the claims. Piecework is now illegal, but the Department has proposed a new system in which home employers would register with the Department, providing it with lists of workers so that on-the-spot inspections can be made. They feel that fair employers should be allowed to operate.

The ILGWU feels that piecework at home cannot be monitored effectively, and would prefer that the government restriction against it remain in effect.

5. The ILGWU favors strict government control of working conditions because

(1) their union would gain power
(2) poor people will always be exploited
(3) Bordeaux, Inc., would grow
(4) the minimum wage will rise
(5) the minimum wage will remain the same

6. The Labor Department sees the main cause of the dispute as

(1) labor vs. management
(2) unions vs. unorganized labor
(3) responsible vs. irresponsible management
(4) sweatshops vs. piece workers
(5) ILGWU vs. Bordeaux, Inc.

Check your answers to the GED Mini-Test on page 93.

Answers and Explanations

Practice *pp. 89–90*

1. Answer: (2) This is the best choice from the last sentence in the first paragraph. Choices (1) and (3) are not stated or assumed; choices (4) and (5) relate to other aspects of poverty.

2. Answer: (2) This is the best choice because the entire passage is about income. Choice (3) is true, but is not a reason; choices (1) and (4) are neither stated nor implied; choice (5) is an opinion.

3. **Answer:** (1)   This is correct from information in the second paragraph. Choice (2) is false; choices (3), (4) and (5) are not supported.

4. **Answer:** (5)   This question asks you to reason from information in the paragraph. If the poor become poorer, what would they be most likely to do? They would probably not become more conservative, choice (1), or more idealistic, choice (4). Choice (2) is not a political effect. Between choices (3) and (5), pick choice (5). People try to affect the government when they are not satisfied with it.

5. **Answer:** (5)   When asked a main idea question, try to bring all the information together. In this cartoon, labor, management and the press are all involved. Choices (1), (2), (3) and (4) are all concerned with details and not the main idea.

6. **Answer:** (2)   Again, bring all the details of the cartoon together. Choice (1) is a possible outcome but ignores the graphic information (negotiators sleeping). Choice (3) is an opinion. Choices (4) and (5) are not supported.

7. **Answer:** (2)   Suing is a legal action; the item indicates judicial review. Choice (1) was an activity occurring before the suing. Choices (3) and (5) may or may not have occurred. Choice (4) is being tried for the same crime twice.

8. **Answer:** (5)   This question asks you to determine effect. The people most hurt by closing the ports are the people dependent on the port: importers whose goods pass through the port.

GED Mini-Test *pp. 91–92*

1. **Answer:** (2)   This is correct from the main idea of the text and from the questions in the third paragraph. Choices (1) and (3) are contradicted; choices (4) and (5) are not supported.

2. **Answer:** (4)   This is the best choice from the emphasis on education throughout the text. Choice (1) is a distractor from the information on fast foods; choices (2) and (3) might be indicated by the information on black female unemployment, but are not supported by the author; choice (5) would not help teenagers to get jobs.

3. **Answer:** (3)   This is the best choice from the second paragraph. Choices (1), (2), (4) and (5) are all possible answers, but are not specifically indicated by the author.

4. **Answer:** (4)   This is an individual personality characteristic; the government cannot control it. However, the government can control choice (1) by law, choices (2) and (3) by public education and social welfare programs and choice (5) by controlling the amount of money in the economy and by mandating government programs like the Civilian Conservation Corps and CETA.

5. **Answer:** (2)   People who have little money or power need a strong voice to protect their rights. There is no basis in the article for choices (1), (4) and (5). Choice (3) is false because the ILGWU is interested in protecting workers' rights, not the corporation's.

6. **Answer:** (3)   The passage states that the Labor Department is searching for a way to allow fair employers to operate, while penalizing exploitative employers. Choices (1) and (2) do not reflect the Labor Department's view. Choice (4) is incorrect; the passage states that sweatshop and piecework are similar. Choice (5) is a true dispute, but does not state the *main cause* of the dispute.

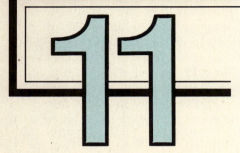

Government and Economics

Government influence on the economy has increased as government spending and government regulation of economic activity have grown over the years.

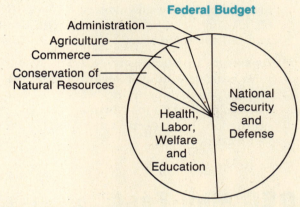

Federal Budget

- Administration
- Agriculture
- Commerce
- Conservation of Natural Resources
- Health, Labor, Welfare and Education
- National Security and Defense

The U.S. government spends more money and has a larger payroll than any business in the world. Its budget runs into billions of dollars. Almost 50% of the federal budget is directly related to the national security and defense; a third is spent on health, labor, welfare and education; and the rest is divided among conservation of natural resources, agriculture, commerce and administration. Expanding, restricting and directing the amount of government spending affects the economy.

Whenever there is spending, there must be income. Government spending is paid for by citizens' and corporations' taxes. The federal income tax pays for federal spending. Traditionally the federal income tax has been a graduated income tax: People with higher incomes pay a higher proportion of their income to the government in taxes; people with lower incomes pay a lower percentage of their income in taxes.

Local government spending is paid for by local taxes, often a property tax or a sales tax. Both property and sales taxes are fixed percentage taxes. Property owners pay a fixed percentage of the value of their property to the government each year. The sales tax is sometimes applied to all products sold; it is sometimes applied to only luxury items, not necessities like food or clothing.

For citizens to be taxed, they also must have income, or money coming into the household. This income may be salaries or wages from employment, interest or dividends from investments, rental income from properties, small business income or transfer payments from the government. Transfer payments are *not* payments for work performed, but benefits like welfare or Medicaid.

In this century the government has steadily increased its control of the economy through regulation. It limits monopolies, regulates interstate commerce, restricts or expands the amount of money in the economy, uses the Federal Reserve System as a central bank and sets up international trade agreements.

Through spending, taxation and regulation, the government touches the economic life of every citizen.

Assess the Adequacy of Data to Support Conclusions

This skill involves applying information in charts, graphs or a written passage to prove or disprove statements.

To assess the accuracy and **adequacy** of facts, follow these steps:

1. *Look for supporting details in the text.* Support may be in graphic form (chart, table, graph, picture, cartoon) or in words. Quotations from an expert or reference to a document are also ways an author can provide supporting details.
2. *Make a list of these details.* This list will help you to determine if the data proves or disproves a statement (conclusion).
3. *Study the internal logic and the accuracy of the statement (conclusion).* Ask yourself, Is it logical? Is it correct and accurate? Does the data support or disprove the conclusion? If yes, then the data is adequate. If no, then the data is insufficient or the conclusion is inaccurate.

Examples

DIRECTIONS: Use the information on this and the preceding page to choose the <u>one</u> best answer for each item below.

1. Thomas Jefferson said "that government governs best which governs least." Modern Americans seem to disagree. They have chosen a government which

   (1) spends a lot of money
   (2) taxes all its citizens
   (3) is increasingly regulatory
   (4) pervades every aspect of life
   (5) taxes luxury items

Answer: (3) This example asks you to decide which answer choice supports disagreement with Thomas Jefferson. Jefferson believed in government which governed as little as possible. Disagreement indicates government which governs as much as possible. That government would be increasingly regulatory.

2. The type of business *most* influenced by the government budget is

   (1) secretarial
   (2) agricultural
   (3) child care
   (4) publishing
   (5) defense related

Answer: (5) The supporting detail in the text is "almost 50% of the federal budget is related to national security and defense." Any increases or decreases in the federal budget are most likely to affect businesses very dependent on the budget, that is, defense-related businesses.

Practice

HINT Remember, a fact is a statement that can be proved. An opinion is a statement of belief that cannot be proved. Be aware of the difference between them when you read a passage.

DIRECTIONS: Choose the one best answer for each item below.

Items 1–4 refer to the following passage.

Secretary of Defense Weinberger reported in 1985 that the United States industrial base was experiencing a decline in both civilian and military areas. At the same time the Soviet Union was rapidly expanding its industrial base, which is dedicated to producing arms. An indicator of the decline in industrialization is a 16% decline in steel production. Steel is a necessary material for most heavy industries. Furthermore, the United States is more than 50% dependent on foreign imports for 19 important minerals. Unless the United States rethinks its economic strategy it will fall far behind in the arms race. The United States must develop a protectionist position for its own economic and military health.

1. Why is the decline in steel production an indication of a decline in industrialization?

   (1) Steel is used for defense.
   (2) Steel is a strong material.
   (3) Many basic industries use steel.
   (4) The U.S. imports steel.
   (5) Steel is used to protect U.S. trade.

2. The author of the above passage would be *most* likely to agree with the statement that the U.S. economy

   (1) is expanding too rapidly
   (2) depends too much on foreign imports
   (3) is too protectionist
   (4) makes too much steel
   (5) is stronger than Russia's

3. Which detail *best* supports the conclusion that the U.S. must develop a protectionist attitude toward its own economy?

   (1) Russia manufactures many arms.
   (2) Steel production went down 16%.
   (3) Steel production is a basic industry.
   (4) The U.S. is behind in the arms race.
   (5) The U.S. imports more than 50% of 19 important minerals.

4. Legislators who agree with the ideas presented in the text above would

   (1) pass laws encouraging development of basic industries
   (2) encourage more trade with Southeast Asia
   (3) pass laws allowing more cheap imports
   (4) go on fact-finding missions to Russia
   (5) discourage financial incentives for defense industries

GO ON TO THE NEXT PAGE.

5. Budget legislation promised a balanced budget by cutting down on government spending. One effect of this legislation would be

(1) more support for Star Wars defense plans
(2) higher taxes for people in every tax bracket
(3) more financial support for public education
(4) less financial support for welfare programs
(5) less income for the government

6. In 1980 Chrysler Corporation, the tenth largest company in the United States, faced bankruptcy. Congress voted to back up loans made to Chrysler by private banks. Which is the *most* probable reason for Congress' support?

(1) United States' citizens need cars.
(2) More cars would increase oil sales.
(3) Chrysler is an American institution.
(4) Chrysler's closing would create massive unemployment.
(5) Congress always aids corporations in financial difficulty.

7. The National Debt reached a peak in the early 1940s. This high debt was caused by

(1) unemployment
(2) taxation
(3) defense spending
(4) budgeting
(5) high-income levels

8. Through 1986, the United States had a graduated income tax which took a larger fraction of income from high-income citizens and a smaller fraction of income from low-income citizens. In practice, the tax law offered many benefits, tax shelters and loopholes to higher income individuals. In 1987 a flat rate income tax with few tax shelters was begun. Why did the Congress pass a flat rate income tax law?

(1) The government needed more money.
(2) The government needed less money.
(3) The graduated income tax was not practiced fairly.
(4) The graduated income tax was too difficult to enforce.
(5) The graduated income tax was hated by the citizens.

9. Tariffs, or taxes, on imported goods are one way of regulating trade by reducing the competition from foreign products. Which of the following products would the government be *most* likely to place a high tariff on?

(1) oil
(2) automobiles
(3) zinc
(4) record albums
(5) sports equipment

10. By 1990 the percentage of Americans thirty years of age or older will have increased to about 55% of the population. The government program *most* affected economically by an aging population would be

(1) Social Security
(2) Welfare
(3) the Federal Housing Authority
(4) the Red Cross
(5) the Department of Vocational Education

Before you take the GED Mini-Test, check your answers on pages 99–100.

GED Mini-Test

DIRECTIONS: Choose the one best answer for each item below.

Items 1–4 refer to the following passage.

In the past shoppers had little protection. Every store should have been posted with large signs saying "Buyer, beware!" If a baker bought flour that was full of weevils, he would have to sift out the bugs, cook with them or toss out the flour and lose his money. If a commuter bought a car with brakes that did not work well, he had to spend his weekends fixing the car himself or pay a garage for repairs.

Now public awareness of consumer rights, increased federal regulation, public relations on the part of manufacturers and store owners and self-policing by various groups have combined to increase consumer protection. Most large groceries will replace food that has gone stale or sour, and, in fact, include the cost of returns in the amount of mark-up on groceries. Car manufacturers recall automobiles that have defects that put the driver at risk.

1. What has caused the increase in consumer protection over time?

   (1) danger to the public safety
   (2) smart public relations
   (3) decreased government regulation
   (4) consumer and corporate concern and government regulation
   (5) lobbying by the agricultural interests in the country

2. Which of the following is the *best* example of industry self-policing for consumer protection?

   (1) listing of ingredients on groceries
   (2) rating of movies by the Motion Picture Association of America
   (3) state laws on seat belts
   (4) 7/11 stores removing pornographic magazines from public shelves
   (5) comparison testing in advertisements

3. Which of the following is the *best* example of government regulation for consumer protection?

   (1) listing of ingredients on groceries
   (2) rating of movies by the Motion Picture Association of America
   (3) wearing dark glasses when skiing
   (4) 7/11 stores removing pornographic magazines from public shelves
   (5) comparison testing in advertisements

4. The manufacturer's cost of recalling defective merchandise is probably paid for by the

   (1) government
   (2) manufacturer
   (3) automobile industry
   (4) consumer
   (5) labor union

GO ON TO THE NEXT PAGE.

5. Traditionally, economists have thought that consumer desires governed the market. One way in which the corporation or manufacturer helps to direct consumer desires and increase consumer demand is

    (1) product design
    (2) advertising
    (3) public image
    (4) market research
    (5) good worker relations

6. Recent malpractice cases against doctors have cost insurance companies millions of dollars. Some students have sued public and private universities for not training the students appropriately; the students have not been able to get jobs. In these examples consumer protection covers

    (1) products
    (2) processes
    (3) services
    (4) systems
    (5) insurance

Check your answers to the GED Mini-Test on page 100.

Answers and Explanations

Practice *pp. 96–97*

1. **Answer:** (3) This is correct because it logically supports the connection between decline in steel production and decline in industrialization. Choices (1) and (2) are true, but do not support the relationship between the decline in industrialization and the decline in steel production. From the information given you cannot know whether choice (4) is correct or incorrect. Choice (5) does not make sense.

2. **Answer:** (2) This is the best choice if you follow the author's argument. He argues that the U.S. economy needs to be protected because it depends heavily on foreign imports for important minerals. Therefore, he would not agree with choice (3). He talks about decline rather than expansion, choice (1). He implies that the U.S. economy is weakening in relation to Russia's, but does not give you information on its present position, choice (5). There is no reference to choice (4).

3. **Answer:** (5) This is the best choice because protectionism relieves the dependence on imports by making U.S. production cost-effective. None of the other details relates as closely to the idea of the U.S. protecting its own economy by making it more self-sufficient.

4. **Answer:** (1) The main idea of the passage is that the U.S. economy needs protection in order to reverse the decline in basic industries. Therefore, lawmakers would pass laws encouraging basic industry development. Choices (2) and (3) would increase imports, thus decreasing the industrial base. Choice (4) would not make any difference to basic industries. Choice (5) would probably work against basic industries.

5. **Answer:** (4) This is the best choice because it would cut government spending. Choices (1) and (3) would increase spending. Choices (2) and (5) relate to government income, not spending.

6. **Answer:** (4) Note that Chrysler is the tenth largest company in the United States. If Chrysler plants closed, jobs would also be lost by salesmen, advertisers and other support industries. Hundreds of thousands of employees and their families would be affected. Choice (1) is faulty logic; other types of cars would still be available. Choices (2) and (3) are accurate statements but would not influence a Congressional action. Choice (5) is false.

7. **Answer:** (3) This is the best choice. National debt is high when government spending is high without adequate income from taxation. U.S. participation in World War II began in the early 1940s. The government had to finance a larger army and produce many weapons for the U.S. and its allies. Choice (1) might increase spending, but unemployment was low in the early 1940s because many were involved in the war effort. Choice (2) increases income, not spending. Choice (4) equalizes income and spending. Choice (5) has nothing to do with the National Debt.

8. **Answer:** (3) This is correct from information about tax shelters for high-income citizens. No information is given on choices (1) and (2). Choice (4) is a possible inference, but not well supported. Choice (5) is an unsupported opinion.

9. **Answer:** (2) Cars are mass-produced inexpensively in Japan. To keep competition on a par with the American automotive industry, they have a high tariff. Choices (1) and (3) are commodities that the country does not have a large amount of. Their importation would be encouraged. There is a small market for choices (4) and (5), so a high tariff is not needed.

10. **Answer:** (1) Social Security would be the most economically affected because the percentage of people retiring and claiming benefits will be higher than the percentage of people working and contributing benefits. Retirees, on an average, will lead longer lives than retirees of the past. Choices (2), (3) and (5) may feel some economic impact but would not be the most affected. Choice (4) is false by inclusion; the Red Cross is not a government program.

GED Mini-Test *pp. 98–99*

1. **Answer:** (4) This is correct because it brings together the different forces that led to more consumer protection. Choice (1) is an indirect cause; choice (2) is a partial cause; choice (3) is incorrect; choice (5) is not mentioned as a cause.

2. **Answer:** (2) The Motion Picture Association of America was formed by the big film-makers to answer public demand for movie ratings that would protect young viewers from seeing extremely violent or sexual scenes. Choice (4) might seem a reasonable answer, but the seller 7/11 is not in the same industry as the magazine publisher.

3. **Answer:** (1) The Federal Drug Administration requires listing of food additives on groceries. Therefore, this is an example of government regulating consumer protection. There is no government participation in the other choices.

4. **Answer:** (4) This answer is implied by the statement that grocery stores often pass the cost of returned merchandise on to the consumer in their mark-up. No other choice is supported or implied in the text.

5. **Answer:** (2) Advertising is designed to sell a product by appealing to the consumer. Advertising often creates a demand for a new product. Choice (4) is a possible answer, but market research usually *measures* consumer demand; it does not direct it.

6. **Answer:** (3) Both the medical profession and education are services.

The most important thing to remember about economics is that economics studies relationships. You have studied the relationships between money and goods and services, production and distribution of goods and services, prices and costs, labor and management, government and business, the corporation and the consumer. Whenever you read an article on economics, try to discover a pattern or relationship in the text. Try to determine whether things go up together, down together or have an inverse relationship in which one item goes up, or increases, while the other item goes down, or decreases. Look for **chronological order:** *What happens first, second, third* and *fourth.* Ask whether there is a cause and effect relationship. Whenever you find a graph or chart or table about economics, find out what sort of pattern is defined.

DIRECTIONS: Choose the one best answer for each item below.

Items 1–4 refer to the following passage.

A recent idea in economics is the wage-price spiral. Increasing wages through union negotiations increases prices. Large corporations insist on maintaining their profits. If wages go up, the increase in cost of production is passed on to the consumer as an increase in cost of the item. Since the corporation continues to profit, labor, through union negotiation, demands even higher wages. Again production costs go up and consumer cost goes up. The net result is inflation. Unions oppose limiting wage increases while corporations refuse to limit price increases.

1. An economist who wanted to stop the wage-price spiral would probably advocate

   (1) unionization
   (2) higher profits
   (3) government control of prices
   (4) socialism
   (5) price increases

2. ___?___ would be against wage control and ___?___ would be against price control.

   (1) Consumers; labor
   (2) Unions; consumers
   (3) Manufacturers; unions
   (4) Consumers; corporations
   (5) Labor; corporations

3. Escalation of the wage-price spiral would result in

   (1) too little money in the economy
   (2) too much money in the economy
   (3) rising prices
   (4) lowering prices
   (5) labor-management confrontations

4. The wage-price spiral would *not* exist in

   (1) an industrial economy
   (2) a capitalist economy
   (3) an agrarian economy
   (4) a communist economy
   (5) a manufacturing economy

GO ON TO THE NEXT PAGE.

5. A barter economy is one in which goods and services are exchanged without using money. Which of the following is the *best* example of a barter economy?

(1) return of a defective item
(2) exchanging a birthday present
(3) a manufacturer's rebate
(4) a baby-sitting co-op
(5) an automated-teller machine

6. OSHA, the Occupational Safety and Health Act, regulates safety in the work place. This is an example of government protection of the

(1) employer
(2) employee
(3) consumer
(4) corporation
(5) legislator

Items 7–10 refer to the following passage.

Congress has created several regulatory commissions that protect citizens from certain problems of economic life. These regulatory commissions affect banking, transportation, labor unions, communication and business corporations. Regulatory commissions enact rules and mediate or arbitrate disputes between opposing parties.

One example of a regulatory commission is the Federal Communications Commission, or FCC. The FCC licenses all radio and television stations. It decides on broadcasting wavelengths and channels.

The basis on which it makes decisions is whether "public convenience, interest or necessity" is well served. If the FCC thinks that a radio or television station is not operating for the public benefit, it can take back the station's license. Then the station can no longer broadcast.

When Congress establishes a regulatory commission, it makes sure that the commission is independent. The president is not allowed to fire commission members or chairmen. In this way Congress keeps the regulatory commissions from satisfying the political goals of a party or president. Instead the commission is free to continue to regulate economic activity in the public interest.

7. Why were regulatory commissions formed by Congress?

(1) Citizens had too much control over their economic life.
(2) The economy was depressed.
(3) The president felt it was important.
(4) Large areas of the economy were operating against the public interest.
(5) Congress was overwhelmed by economic problems.

8. Whether an advertisement abides by the "truth in advertising" rules is probably determined by

(1) Congress
(2) the president
(3) a commission
(4) a TV station
(5) the consumer

9. A regulatory commission would probably rule in a dispute between

(1) a public-interest group and a toy manufacturer
(2) Congress and the president
(3) a TV station and an advertiser
(4) two political parties
(5) a supermarket and a consumer

10. Which of the following is the *best* conclusion to draw about the effect of regulatory commissions on the economy?

(1) They expand the economy.
(2) They restrict the economy.
(3) They intervene in the operation of corporations.
(4) They intervene in the operation of the open market.
(5) They cause products to be less expensive.

GO ON TO THE NEXT PAGE.

Items 11–12 refer to the following cartoon.

"Made in Hong Kong! Made in Hong Kong! How can we compete with their cheap labor?"

11. An appropriate government response to protect the U.S. economy in the situation pictured would be to

   (1) increase sales taxes
   (2) increase export quotas
   (3) institute price controls
   (4) increase import tariffs
   (5) advertise "Buy American!"

12. The *most* probable solution to the situation pictured in the cartoon is to

   (1) buy more radios
   (2) buy radios made in the U.S.
   (3) buy radios made in Hong Kong
   (4) avoid buying radios
   (5) buy televisions instead of radios

13. A new federal tax bill canceled the deductions for sales taxes beginning on January 1, 1987. Economists predicted that

   (1) consumers would buy even more at Christmastime
   (2) manufacturers would produce less at the end of the year
   (3) the new year would see a growth in sales
   (4) consumers would wait on buying more expensive items like dishwashers
   (5) department stores would cancel their New Year sales discounts

14. Federal broadcast deregulation relieves local television stations of the obligation to present news and public affairs programs. News and public affairs programs have generally been unprofitable. Television station response is *most* likely to be to

   (1) increase news programming
   (2) replace news programming with public affairs discussions
   (3) replace national news programs with local news programs
   (4) replace news programs with more profitable programs
   (5) make no change in their schedules

Items 15–16 refer to the following definitions.

Movement of the economy is classified by many different terms that explain the effects that wages, production and cost-of-living expenses have on each other at a given time. Listed below are five of these terms and brief descriptions of the economic trends they indicate.

   (1) **Inflation**—A continuing rise in the prices of goods and services
   (2) **Demand-pull inflation**—Caused by a demand for goods that are in short supply
   (3) **Cost-push inflation**—Caused by a push for higher wages resulting in higher prices. Also called the wage-price spiral
   (4) **Recession**—A period in which production declines and people have less money
   (5) **Depression**—A severe reduction or slowing of business activity and cash flow

15. When an oil embargo was imposed in the 1970s, Americans had to wait in long lines on alternate days of the week to get fuel for their cars. The prices paid for this fuel demonstrate

   (1) cost-pull inflation
   (2) demand-pull inflation
   (3) inflation
   (4) recession
   (5) depression

16. In 1980 it cost more than $2.00 to purchase an item that had cost less than $1.00 in 1970. This is an example of

   (1) demand-pull inflation
   (2) cost-pull inflation
   (3) inflation
   (4) depression
   (5) recession

Check your answers to the Review on pages 156 .

OVERVIEW
Political Science

A joint session of Congress with spectators in the gallery.

citizen
a member of a society or nation

representative democracy
government by officials elected by the citizens

Human beings live in groups, or societies. Since most individuals are governed by self-interest, they sometimes come into conflict with other people's needs and wishes or with their society as a whole. Human societies usually develop laws, rules made to protect people from one another and to help their society work smoothly for the good of all members. Societies and nations have governments, organized groups of individuals who make laws and have the authority and power to enforce those laws.

The **citizens** of the United States chose a type of government called a representative democracy. A **democracy** is a government in which power is vested in the people. Many people consider a democracy to be "rule by the majority." In a **representative democracy,** power is exercised by the people through their elected representatives. In the United States, citizens elect representatives to many positions in government, such as senators and mayors.

When our nation was founded, many people were concerned about rule by the majority. They feared "mobocracy," or rule by the mob. Consequently, they divided the government into three branches: legislative, executive and judicial. Each of these branches is separate from the others, but exercises some influence on the others. This is called the American system of **checks and balances.**

The **legislative** authority to make laws is given to the **Congress.** The two Houses of Congress are the **Senate,** which has two elected officials from each state, and the **House of Representatives,** which has a number of elected officials from each state depending on the state's population.

The laws that the Congress passes are enforced by the **executive** branch of government. The executive is headed by the president, elected by all the citizens through the electoral college. The president appoints members of his cabinet, like the attorney-general and the secretary of state, to help him with his duties. Presidents, with the help of Congress, have also formed specialized departments and offices to perform specific functions of government.

The **judicial** branch has the power to decide cases in courts of law. The Supreme Court is the highest court in the land. Congress has also established a system of lower or inferior courts. In order to protect the independence of the judicial branch, the Constitution allows judges to be appointed for life as long as they are innocent of any illegal actions. One important aspect of the system of checks and balances is the power of judicial review. Judicial review is the court power to judge the constitutionality of a specific law. If the court decides that a law goes against or beyond the powers delegated to the federal government or states in the Constitution, it will rule that law unconstitutional, and, therefore, invalid.

The United States is a great experiment in democracy. Citizens participate at all levels of government. Through the separation of powers in the three branches of government, the U.S. insures that the government works for the welfare of all, and not for the good of special interest groups.

checks and balances
the system that keeps the branches of government from getting too powerful

legislative
law-making branch of government

Senate
one of the two houses of Congress

House of Representatives
one of the two houses of Congress

executive
law-enforcing branch of government consisting of the president and cabinet

judicial
law-dispensing branch of government consisting of the courts

12 American Politics

The American political system began in an act of rebellion. It continued because Americans were willing to compromise and negotiate.

On July 4, Americans celebrate Independence Day. Our country began as colonies, subject to the English king's government. Early Americans were not happy with the king's right to tax and to control their trade when they had no representation or voice in their own government. These dissatisfactions peaked in the Declaration of Independence, a revolutionary step in world government.

The Declaration of Independence was unique in stating that:

1. All men were created equal.
2. Government governed only by consent of the governed.
3. The people have the right to abolish or change their form of government.

Once Americans declared independence from England, they faced the task of creating a new government. Their first attempt, the Articles of Confederation, allowed each of the thirteen states to keep their own **sovereignty**, or self-government. Under the Articles of Confederation, the state governments only came together to make treaties, declare war or peace, regulate trade with the Indians and establish a postal system. Americans were so afraid of a strong central government after their experience with England that they refused to create a government that could tax or make laws easily.

The Articles of Confederation did not work. Americans did not present a united front to the rest of the world, especially France and England. Their money had little value because each state printed its own currency, not valuable in the other states.

Finally, representatives from the state governments, except Rhode Island, met again to write the Constitution of the United States. The Constitution is a great compromise between:

1. A strong central government and state sovereignty
2. Equal representation for all states and representation based on population
3. Ways of counting slaves, people who were owned by others (already a controversial issue in colonial times), for purposes of taxation and representation

One brilliant idea the writers of the Constitution had was to include in the Constitution a process for changing or amending this document. In this way, as the country changed and developed, the government could also change and develop.

Distinguish Fact from Opinion

This skill involves determining which statements can be proved.

A statement of **fact** can always be checked. It can be proved or disproved. Fact in a passage is usually followed by details that support the statement.

A statement of **opinion** cannot be checked. It expresses what someone thinks or believes is true. Some clue words to opinions are: comparatives like good, better, best or bad, worse, worst, expressions like absolutely, certainly, obviously, which ask the reader to accept a statement without thinking about it. Other cue words are those that indicate emotion like afraid, cowardly and brave.

Remember:

1. **Facts** can be checked; they are supported by details.
2. **Opinions** cannot be checked; they are emotional statements of belief.

Examples

DIRECTIONS: Use the information on this and the preceding page to choose the <u>one</u> best answer for each item below.

1. Which of the following is an example of an author's opinion?

   (1) On July 4, Americans celebrate Independence Day.
   (2) The Declaration of Independence was unique.
   (3) Americans faced the task of creating a new government.
   (4) Americans were afraid of a strong central government.
   (5) Representatives met to write the Constitution of the U.S.

   Answer: (4) This is an opinion because it is too general a statement to check. Some, not all, Americans may have been afraid. Choices (1), (2), (3) and (5) can all be checked by reference to a history book.

2. The idea that the Constitution is a great compromise is supported by the fact that the U.S. government has

   (1) the power to tax
   (2) the Senate and the House of Representatives
   (3) a standing army
   (4) abolished slavery
   (5) a Supreme Court with nine justices

   Answer: (2) This is correct because the Senate has equal representation for the states and the House of Representatives has representation based on population, a compromise mentioned in the text.

Practice

Analyze a chain of events or sequence of facts to determine whether a hypothesis is supported or a conclusion is justified. GED test items should always be answered by *logic*, not *opinion*.

DIRECTIONS: Choose the <u>one</u> best answer for each item below.

Items 1–8 refer to the following passage.

The Constitution of the United States divides governing power among three branches: legislative, executive and judicial. While each branch is separate, a system of **checks and balances,** where one branch has influence or power over another, was put into effect.

Legislative power to make laws is held by Congress: the Senate with two delegates from each state and the House with a proportional number of delegates based on the population of each state. Congress was delegated many important powers, including the power to tax, borrow money, regulate foreign and interstate trade, coin money and punish counterfeiters, establish a post office and declare war. Congress as a whole has the right to make laws for the United States, but only the House of Representatives may initiate bills for raising money.

Executive power to enforce the laws is held by the president. He is also commander-in-chief of the armed forces. He can make Supreme Court appointments with Senate approval.

The Supreme Court and lower courts have **judicial power** to settle disputes or cases in courts of law. The Supreme Court has original jurisdiction, or first hearing, of cases involving conflicts between states or foreign diplomats. All other cases are first heard in lower courts, but may go to the Supreme Court on appeal.

1. A decision to send military advisers to a country experiencing internal political problems would probably be made by

   (1) the Supreme Court
   (2) the Senate
   (3) the Congress
   (4) the House of Representatives
   (5) the president

2. A decision to no longer trade with a foreign country that disagreed with U.S. policy would probably be made by

   (1) the Supreme Court
   (2) the Senate
   (3) the Congress
   (4) the House of Representatives
   (5) the president

GO ON TO THE NEXT PAGE.

3. Which of the following cases would fall under the original jurisdiction of the Supreme Court?

(1) boundary dispute between U.S. and Canada
(2) boundary dispute between two states
(3) dispute about import tariffs
(4) drunk driving charge against the son of a diplomat
(5) case against a counterfeiter

4. Which of the following is the *best* reason why the House, rather than the Senate, was given the right to initiate bills on taxation?

(1) The House is larger than the Senate.
(2) Senators are more important than Representatives.
(3) The vice-president presides in the House of Representatives.
(4) The U.S. population is represented more accurately by the House.
(5) Taxation is the most important issue before Congress.

5. How is the fact that the census is taken every ten years important to the legislative branch of government?

(1) redrawing state boundaries
(2) determining representation in the House
(3) deciding how many senators each state has
(4) deciding how much money has to be collected in taxes
(5) determining how many people to draft into the army

6. Supreme Court justices hold their offices for life. A president can use his power to appoint Supreme Court justices to

(1) make the views of the Court closer to his own
(2) change a specific court ruling
(3) pack the court with conservatives
(4) enable the judicial and executive branch to work together
(5) fire all the justices

7. The separation of government into three branches allows for a system of checks and balances in which one branch of government has review over another. An example of checks and balances is

(1) presidential power to veto acts of Congress
(2) original jurisdiction of the Supreme Court
(3) House power to write tax bills
(4) Senate power to create committees
(5) president's role as commander-in-chief

8. How can Congress act to limit the president's role as commander-in-chief of the armed forces?

(1) filibuster
(2) refuse to appropriate money for military spending
(3) refuse to increase taxes
(4) vote against his role as commander-in-chief
(5) declare war

Before you take the GED Mini-Test, check your answers on pages 111–112.

PRACTICE   109

TIP

If you skip a question, keep track on your answer sheet of where you are. Be sure to correctly place your answer to each test item next to its corresponding test item number.

DIRECTIONS: Choose the one best answer for each item below.

Items 1–2 refer to the following passage.

The Bill of Rights, the first ten amendments to the Constitution, was written by the First Congress at the request of the states. These amendments include individual rights to religious and political freedom, right to bear arms, right to jury trial, right to bail and protection from search and seizure. The Tenth Amendment reserves to the states and the people all rights not given to the United States in the Constitution.

1. In general, the Bill of Rights protects

   (1) national rights
   (2) state rights
   (3) citizen rights
   (4) local government rights
   (5) federal rights

2. Which power does the Bill of Rights limit?

   (1) federal government
   (2) state government
   (3) local government
   (4) county government
   (5) city government

Items 3–4 refer to the following passage.

Local government is responsible for providing many different services. The most expensive item in the local budget is education. Nearly one-third of all state and local revenue is spent on schools. Local government also offers police protection, road building and repair, and sewage, sanitation and public welfare services.

Local government is usually paid for by a property tax. The property tax is a percentage tax on real estate owned in the city or country. It yields a lot of money, is easy to collect, and can be raised to provide more revenue, if necessary.

3. The property tax as a method of raising money for local government falls *most* unfairly on

   (1) families
   (2) non-profit organizations
   (3) homeowners
   (4) the elderly
   (5) the rich

4. A local government wants to attract revenue without raising the amount of money spent on services. Which will it promote?

   (1) multi-family housing
   (2) single-family housing
   (3) industrial parks
   (4) apartment buildings
   (5) low-income housing

GO ON TO THE NEXT PAGE.

5. In December 1985 the Housing and Urban Development Department director told city officials that President Reagan had decided to delay spending 3.2 billion dollars in community development block grant funds. San Francisco had to cut community development funds by 32%. This is an example of

(1) state-federal interdependence
(2) financial independence of cities
(3) local dependence on federal monies
(4) interdependence of local and state governments
(5) state independence of federal government

6. In the 1970s and 1980s large numbers of Americans moved from the Snow Belt (northern cities and towns) to the Sun Belt (southwest cities and towns). The political effect caused by this shift in population was *most* strongly felt in the

(1) Democratic and Republican Parties
(2) mayoral elections
(3) Congress
(4) Senate
(5) House of Representatives

Check your answers to the GED Mini-Test on page 112.

Answers and Explanations

Practice *pp. 108–109*

1. Answer: (5)   This is correct because the president as commander-in-chief could send advisors even though war had not been declared. Choice (3), and choices (2) and (4), as houses of Congress, would have to agree to send military troops in an active, not advisory, role. Choice (1) has nothing to do with military decisions.

2. Answer: (3)   This is correct because both houses of Congress would rule on a foreign trade decision. It is not a power assigned to a specific house of Congress, choices (2) and (4). Choices (1) and (5) do not make trade decisions, although the president could ask Congress to refuse to trade with a country.

3. Answer: (2)   This is correct from information in the text. Original jurisdiction applies to disputes between the states or foreign diplomats. Choice (4) is not a diplomat. Choice (1) would be decided by an international court. Choices (3) and (5) would be heard in lower courts.

4. Answer: (4)   This question asks you to think about differences between the House and Senate and how those differences relate to decisions on taxation. The U.S. population as a whole is taxed, so the legislators who represent them the best in terms of numbers should initiate tax legislation. Choices (2) and (5) are opinion statements. Choice (1) is true, but not a reason why the House initiates tax laws. Choice (3) is false.

5. Answer: (2)   You must consider relationships between the census, a count of population, and the legislature. Choice (2) is correct because numbers of representatives change when the numbers of state residents change. Choices (1) and (3) have already been decided. Choices (4) and (5) are not legislative decisions, although census information may be relevant for these decisions.

6. Answer: (1)   This is the best choice because the president does have the option to appoint new justices when a justice dies or retires. A president will try to bring the Court into line with his views as a way of influencing the judiciary branch. Choice (4) is a second-best answer; the judiciary and the executive already work together, although they may not always agree. Choice (2) would not be possible since justices are appointed for life. Choice (3) is an opinion since some presidents would be liberal and could try to appoint liberal judges. Choice (5) is false from information in the item.

7. Answer: (1)   From the item you are looking for an example in which one branch of government affects another. Choices (2), (3), (4) and (5) are all situations with reference to only one branch of government.

8. Answer: (2)   From the text you can see that Congress has a strong role where money is concerned. Choice (1) is a delay tactic only. Choice (3) does not apply specifically to the president's role. Choice (4) could be changed only by amendment to the Constitution. Choice (5) would increase the president's role as commander-in-chief by moving the U.S. into a state of war.

GED Mini-Test   *pp. 110–111*

1. Answer: (3)   This is correct because the majority of the rights listed are individual or citizen rights. The Bill of Rights was written because the states wanted to be sure that the United States government would not have the amount of power that the contemporary European governments had over their citizens.

2. Answer: (1)   This is correct because the Bill of Rights asserts the rights of states and individual citizens. Consequently, it limits federal power.

3. Answer: (4)   This question asks you who bears the burden of taxation without receiving a proportional amount of services. The elderly pay, often out of fixed and limited incomes, but do not receive educational benefits, which are the most expensive. Choice (1) receive a lot of services even when they pay a lot of taxes. Choice (2) are not taxed. Choice (3) may or may not receive educational services. Choice (5) would be a possible answer, but they may receive a lot of services and it is easier for them to pay property taxes than for most elderly people.

4. Answer: (3)   You are asked to judge who will provide revenue without using a proportional amount of services. Industrial parks use a lot of property that can be taxed, but they do not need any educational services provided. Choices (1), (2), (4) and (5) all increase the services required from the local government, even though choices (1), (2) and (4) would probably increase revenue.

5. Answer: (3)   You are asked to analyze a monetary relationship between levels of government. A presidential- or federal-level decision not to release money caused a cut in city or local spending. This is a dependent relationship because it goes in one direction only; it is not an interdependent or two-way relationship. So choice (3) is the best answer.

6. Answer: (5)   Seats in the House of Representatives are based on population. Choices (1) and (2) are incorrect. Mayoral races would not be *most* affected; there is no evidence to show that people who change their residence would also change their party loyalty. Choice (3) is incorrect; Congress is a combination of both House and Senate. Choice (4) is incorrect; each state has two Senate seats regardless of population.

13 American Politics

Political parties grew and changed along with the country. The policies and politics that served the citizens of the 1780s are not the same as those that serve the citizens of the 1980s, although they share the same roots.

Since the American Revolution the country has been run, for the most part, by a two-party system.

The struggle over the ratification of the Constitution led to the first two political parties, the **Federalists,** who supported the new Constitution, and the **Anti-Federalists,** who were opposed to it in that form. George Washington was elected into office by the Federalists in 1789. By the election of 1792, Thomas Jefferson headed the **Democratic-Republican** party, which emerged in opposition to the Federalists, who favored a loose, or flexible, interpretation of the Constitution and a strong central government.

Other parties were formed and were either dissolved or absorbed into existing parties. In the election of 1828, Andrew Jackson of Tennessee became president on the **Democratic** ticket, defeating the New Englander, John Quincy Adams, a **National-Republican.** The frontiersman Jackson's victory symbolized the arrival of the "common people" to political power. This is considered the first ticket of the modern Democratic party. The **Republican** party, formed in 1856, became a popular force in 1860 with the election of Abraham Lincoln.

Today the Democratic and Republican parties dominate the political scene. Democrats are considered more liberal, Republicans, more conservative. Some candidates run on the **Independent** ticket; they do not align themselves with either party. Although no Independent party candidates have won a major election, their force has been felt by getting votes that would have otherwise gone to the Republican or Democratic candidates.

Delegates to the 1976 Democratic Convention in New York City.

Use Given Ideas in Another Context

This skill involves taking information you already know and making it work for you in a new situation.

Use the passage on page 113 to ask yourself: What do I already know about political parties in the United States? On a sheet of paper, write three things you know. **1.** There are ___?___ major political parties in the United States. **2.** They are called the ___?___ and the ___?___ parties. **3.** The ___?___ party is usually conservative. The ___?___ party is usually liberal.

   You already know the two major political parties. Add the new facts you are about to read to this base.

Read and connect information   Politicians sometimes find that their beliefs and values develop over time. Some party leaders have actually changed parties in mid-career. Senator Wayne Morse of Oregon and Mayor John Lindsay of New York switched from the Republican to the Democratic party. Senator Strom Thurmond of South Carolina and Governor John Connally of Texas became Republicans after beginning their careers as Democrats. In his years as a leader of the Screen Actors Guild, Ronald Reagan was formerly a Democrat, but when elected Governor of California and President of the United States, he was a Republican.

Examples

DIRECTIONS: Combine the information in the passage above with what you already know to choose the <u>one</u> best answer for each item below.

1. Lindsay probably saw the political climate of New York City as

   (1) changeable
   (2) conservative
   (3) independent
   (4) liberal
   (5) right-wing

Answer: (4)   List *new* facts: Lindsay switched from Republican to Democrat. List *known* facts: Democrat/liberal, Republican/conservative.

2. The *most* likely one to change party affiliation would be a(n)

   (1) liberal Democrat
   (2) right-wing Republican
   (3) conservative Democrat
   (4) conservative Republican
   (5) Independent

Answer: (3)   List *new* facts: People change parties because their ideas and values change. List *known* facts: Democrat/liberal, Republican/conservative.

Practice

HINT ▷ Remember to ask who, what, where, when, why and/or how when reading a passage. This will help you locate new information to build upon the facts you already know.

DIRECTIONS: Choose the one best answer for each item below.

Items 1–4 refer to the following passage.

The Joint Center for Political Studies announced that in 1985 1.3% of elective offices were held by blacks. This is a 6.1% increase over 1984. Including 1,483 women, 6,424 blacks held elective offices. Two important firsts in 1985 were the election of L. Douglas Wilder as lieutenant governor in Virginia and the election of Alyce Clark to the Mississippi legislature. Until 1985, no black had won a major statewide office in the South since Reconstruction. No woman had ever been elected to the legislature in Mississippi. Mississippi, Louisiana, Illinois and Georgia have the most black elected officials while Idaho, Montana, New Hampshire and North Dakota have none.

1. According to the passage, political progress is being made by blacks because

   (1) they are elected to public office
   (2) they gained positions they have not had in 100 years
   (3) a black woman was elected
   (4) the Joint Center for Political Studies announced it
   (5) black men and women hold offices

2. According to the passage, a black candidate seeking political power would probably do well running for

   (1) mayor of a New England town
   (2) governor of a large Northern state
   (3) mayor of a Southwestern city
   (4) governor of a Southern state
   (5) senator from a Northwestern state

3. Which statement is *best* supported by evidence in the reading?

   (1) More black women held public office in 1985 than in 1984.
   (2) North Dakota and New Hampshire have no black residents.
   (3) Black women have little political power in the South.
   (4) Blacks held elected offices during Reconstruction.
   (5) Alyce Clark is a knowledgeable woman.

4. What conclusion about population distribution and elections can be drawn from the paragraph?

   (1) Many black officials are elected in states with scattered black populations.
   (2) Blacks hold elective office in direct proportion to their numbers in the U.S. population.
   (3) More blacks are political now.
   (4) Black women control the vote.
   (5) More blacks are elected in states with large black populations.

GO ON TO THE NEXT PAGE.

Items 5–10 refer to the following passage.

According to the Constitution, the states are responsible for determining who can vote for President and Vice-President of the United States. However, the Fifteenth Amendment (ratified in 1870) extended the right to vote to all men, regardless of race. The Nineteenth Amendment (1920) allowed women to vote. The Twenty-Third Amendment (1961) permitted District of Columbia residents to vote for the president. The Twenty-Fourth Amendment (1964) abolished the poll tax while the 1965 Voting Rights Act abolished literacy tests for voter registration. The Twenty-Sixth Amendment (1971) lowered the voting age, nationwide, to eighteen. Many states still refuse to allow criminals and insane people to vote.

5. Who would *not* have been allowed to vote in a presidential election?

(1) a Yankee farmer in 1800
(2) a Southern black sharecropper in 1860
(3) a Southern woman in 1964
(4) a District of Columbia resident in 1968
(5) a traffic violator in 1984

6. Prior to 1961 which group was *not* permitted to vote for president?

(1) a woman from Missouri
(2) a man from Alabama
(3) an eighty-year-old male
(4) an eighty-year-old female
(5) a District of Columbia resident

7. How have national legislation and Constitutional amendments affected the right to vote?

(1) decreased percentage of people allowed to vote
(2) increased restrictions on right to vote
(3) allowed conservative people to vote
(4) decreased qualification on right to vote
(5) allowed more unqualified people to vote

8. Some states might refuse the right to vote to criminals and the insane because they feel these people

(1) have no rights
(2) do not share the values of good citizens
(3) do not have the mental capacity to understand political issues
(4) would probably not vote even if they were allowed
(5) either cannot perceive, or would not vote for, the common good

9. Which of the following assumptions is incorrect?

(1) The Constitution grants states various powers.
(2) All men can vote according to the Fifteenth Amendment.
(3) All eighteen-year-olds can vote.
(4) The president must be a Democrat.
(5) Amendments to the Constitution provide American citizens with rights that were not conceived of by our forefathers.

10. What conclusion about the relative power of the federal and state governments can be drawn?

(1) The federal government controls the state governments.
(2) The state governments control the federal government.
(3) The federal government has become more powerful.
(4) The state governments have become more powerful.
(5) There has been no change in the relative power.

Before you take the GED Mini-Test, check your answers on page 118.

13

DIRECTIONS: Choose the one best answer for each item below.

Items 1–5 refer to the following passage.

Political parties are one way that citizens can join together to influence government. But political parties must stand for broad, general ideas because they try to get the support of many different people.

Other groups have more focused goals. Workers who organized into labor groups (unions) helped win better working conditions and salaries for all working people. This type of citizen group is called an interest group, and its purpose is to promote the interests and concerns of its members.

One of the methods interest groups use to achieve their goals is called lobbying, which means trying to persuade government leaders to favor certain causes. The word lobbying dates back to the time, in the early days of the government, when lobbyists used to wait in the lobbies of political buildings hoping to get a politician's attention. Today they are at work at all levels of government, all across the country. One criticism of lobbyists is that they often represent an uneven section of the population.

1. A lobbyist is a(n)

(1) product of twentieth-century politics
(2) politician
(3) activist for a group's cause
(4) lawmaker
(5) government employee

2. Which group, according to the definition of *lobby*, would be *most* effective in helping to bring about social change?

(1) a labor union
(2) the Independent party
(3) a school board
(4) a city council
(5) a parent/teacher association

3. One can become a lobbyist by being

(1) appointed by the president
(2) appointed by a political party
(3) voted into office
(4) hired by a special interest group
(5) in lobbies where politicians work

4. One way in which lobbying by the wealthy is controlled is by

(1) outlawing lobbies
(2) limiting contributions to campaign funds
(3) allowing only a few lobbies
(4) making everyone join lobbies
(5) making lobbyists wait in lobbies

5. Which of the following is the *most* likely action of a group lobbying against nuclear disarmament?

(1) meet with a pro-nuclear committee
(3) attend a tax subcommittee
(5) write a newsletter to their congressman explaining their views

(2) report to *Tass*, a Russian news agency
(4) plan to wait in hotel lobbies

GO ON TO THE NEXT PAGE.

6. John F. Kennedy's famous words, "And so, my fellow Americans, ask not what your country can do for you; ask what you can do for your country," are an appeal to citizens to

    (1) act as responsible citizens
    (2) pay their taxes on time
    (3) send a ten-dollar donation to the government
    (4) support his presidency
    (5) use social services

7. Public demonstrations like the demonstrations against the war in Vietnam measure the force of public opinion because people must actively participate in a public action. However, a demonstration does *not* indicate that

    (1) some people feel strongly about the issue
    (2) many people agree with government policy
    (3) there is dissatisfaction with government policy
    (4) Americans have the right to express their opinions
    (5) individuals will act publicly to express their opinions

Check your answers to the GED Mini-Test on page 119.

Answers and Explanations

Practice *pp. 115–116*

1. **Answer:** (2)   This is correct because it pertains to the "important firsts" in the reading. Choices (1) and (3) are true, but not good indicators of political progress. Choice (4) is not relevant. Choice (5) sounds good but may not be true. Many blacks were elected during the Reconstruction.

2. **Answer:** (4)   According to the information in the passage, a Southern state probably has a large black population, and a precedent has been set in Virginia.

3. **Answer:** (4)   Choices (1), (3) and (5) are not supported in the paragraph. Choice (2) is false from general knowledge.

4. **Answer:** (5)   The last sentence in the reading tells where blacks are and are not elected. General knowledge tells you that Mississippi, Louisiana, Illinois and Georgia have large black populations.

5. **Answer:** (2)   The dates show that black men were not allowed to vote until 1870.

6. **Answer:** (5)   Referring to the passage, the Twenty-Third Amendment, passed in 1961, granted District of Columbia residents the right to vote. Choices (1), (2), (3) and (4) all describe people who had the right to vote prior to 1961.

7. **Answer:** (4)   This is a restatement of the main idea—more and more people have been allowed to vote for President.

8. **Answer:** (5)   This applies to both criminals and the insane. Choice (1) is false; choices (2) and (4) are assumptions; choice (3) applies only to the insane.

9. **Answer:** (4)   The president may be elected from any political party. Choice (4) is the only incorrect assumption. All the other choices represent true statements.

10. **Answer:** (3)   The paragraph tells you that the states were originally responsible for determining who could vote. General knowledge tells you that amendments and acts are enforced by the federal government, so conclude that the federal government has become more powerful.

1. **Answer:** (3)   This choice rephrases the definition given in the passage. Choices (1), (2), (4) and (5) are false.

2. **Answer:** (1)   This choice is correct according to the definition. Choice (2) is too broad, or wide-ranging. Choices (3), (4) and (5) are too local, or limited.

3. **Answer:** (4)   Choices (1), (2) and (3) are incorrect. Choice (5) states how lobbyists used to approach politicians in the past century, not now. Note the question states "can become."

4. **Answer:** (2)   Politicians may only accept a regulated amount of campaign funding from individuals and corporations. Choices (1), (3), (4) and (5) are false, from information given in the passage.

5. **Answer:** (5)   Since lobbying, as defined by the passage, means trying to persuade government leaders to favor certain causes, this choice is the best example of an action likely to be undertaken. Although choice (1) is a possibility, it is not the *most* likely action. Choices (2), (3) and (4) are far-fetched and, therefore, not correct.

6. **Answer:** (1)   "Fellow Americans" and "what *you* can do for your country" are clues. Choices (2), (3), (4) and (5) are incorrect as absolutely no reference is made to them in John F. Kennedy's quoted famous words.

7. **Answer:** (2)   This is the only choice that is not a definition of a demonstration. The question asks you to find the one choice that does not describe a demonstration. Therefore, choices (1), (3), (4) and (5), although correct statements, are incorrect because they do not answer the question.

14 Government, General Welfare

The role of the U.S. government in providing for the general welfare of its citizens has greatly expanded in this century.

Early Americans believed that less government was better government. Modern Americans tend to disagree. Early Americans chose to help the poor and elderly through private charities or state programs, while modern Americans use the federal government to provide relief for the poor. The federal government now seems to have an impact on every part of daily life.

The Great Depression of the 1930s was a turning point in the American view of the federal government. The economy was so shattered that private charities and state governments were not able to solve all the problems of the poor. Consequently, they turned to the federal government. President Franklin D. Roosevelt began numerous social welfare programs that continue to affect the lives of Americans today.

The government pays for these extensive programs by **revenues,** income a government receives into the treasury for public use. The federal income tax is the government's largest single source of revenue. This direct tax on individual or corporate incomes falls on every American across the United States.

The government also borrows money from its citizens in order to finance its programs. The Department of the Treasury sells bonds or treasury notes. It pays interest on these securities. The interest that the government pays on its securities is the **national debt,** more than $800 billion. Paying interest on this debt costs about $60 billion a year.

The revenue brought in by the federal government goes back to the people in many ways. It can be paid directly to an individual. For example, Aid to Families with Dependent Children grants are paid directly to families that demonstrate financial need. It can be channeled through the states for disaster relief or as a grant-in-aid to pay for highway construction or urban renewal. The federal government can also spend the money directly on the general welfare. One example would be the defense of the country. The federal government pays for a standing army and defense systems.

Government is paid for by the people. Its major responsibility is to provide for the general welfare of all citizens through the best means at its disposal.

Distinguish Conclusions from Supporting Statements

This skill involves identifying a correct statement that would justify a conclusion. This skill may involve identifying a main idea and supporting details; fact and opinion; cause and effect.

A **conclusion** is a reasoned judgment or generalization made from the facts. **Supporting statements** are the details or facts that lead to the conclusion. To distinguish a conclusion from the supporting statements:

Read for the main idea.   This gives you the framework for the conclusion.

Ask: How is the paragraph or passage organized?   See how the details or supporting statements make a logical pattern.

Ask: What is the author trying to show or prove?   You may have to *infer* a generalization, trend or probable result or effect from the information given to form a conclusion.

Examples

DIRECTIONS: Use the information on this and the preceding page to choose the one best answer for each item below.

1. The information that early Americans preferred less government and modern Americans prefer more government supports the conclusion that the

   (1) federal government's power is increasing
   (2) state government's power is increasing
   (3) individual's rights are ignored
   (4) revenues are government income
   (5) federal government's role in the U.S. has lessened

Answer: (1)   The comparison between early and late Americans indicates that government's role has expanded.

2. Which statement supports the conclusion that the major responsibility of government is to provide for the general welfare of its people?

   (1) Personal income tax is collected.
   (2) The income tax is the largest source of government revenue.
   (3) Early Americans believed in less government.
   (4) Roosevelt began many welfare programs.
   (5) Government revenue returns to the people through many programs.

Answer: (5)   This supports the idea that government works for the people. It is the only choice that supports the statement.

Practice

HINT ▷ To distinguish a conclusion from supporting statements, look for clue words in each test item. These words indicate a question that asks you to draw a conclusion: generalization, trend, conclude, effect, result. These words ask you to find supporting statements: reason, why, support, indications that, details.

DIRECTIONS: Choose the <u>one</u> best answer for each item below.

1. One clause in the Constitution of the United States reads, "The Congress shall have power to . . . provide for the common defense and general welfare of the United States." This clause has been used to justify

    (1) ratification of treaties
    (2) increases in bureaucracy
    (3) growth of the economy
    (4) government welfare programs
    (5) Star Wars

2. A protective tariff is a tax placed on an imported good to make it more expensive than a locally produced item. A protective tariff on leather would be supported by

    (1) farmers
    (2) shoe manufacturers
    (3) ranchers
    (4) consumers
    (5) handbag manufacturers

3. Many Americans are worried about the $800 billion national debt. In order to reduce the debt the government would have to create a budgetary surplus; it would have to collect more money than it spent. It could do this by

    (1) cutting taxes and increasing welfare programs
    (2) cutting taxes and cutting costs
    (3) raising taxes and increasing welfare programs
    (4) raising taxes and cutting expensive programs
    (5) increasing borrowing and not changing expenditures

4. Protectionism, the practice of providing economic protection for domestic producers by increasing the cost of business to foreign competitors, often favors a group of producers at the expense of consumers. How can protectionism be justified as helping the general welfare?

    (1) More expensive products have better quality.
    (2) Without protectionism, American business and jobs would be lost.
    (3) Consumers deserve to pay more.
    (4) The American economy cannot stand on its own two feet.
    (5) Producers have more political power than consumers.

GO ON TO THE NEXT PAGE.

Items 5–8 refer to the following passage.

In 1913 the Federal Reserve Act established the Federal Reserve System. The Federal Reserve System divides the United States into twelve banking districts; each district has a Federal Reserve Bank. These banks act as bankers to commercial banks by assisting in check collections, furnishing currency and lending money. They also hold commercial bank **reserves,** a minimum amount of funds that each federally chartered bank is required to deposit with the Federal Reserve System.

The Federal Reserve System is the government's banker. It buys and sells gold for the government and it cooperates with the Treasury Department in issuing currency and managing the public debt.

The Federal Reserve System plays an important role in assuring a stable economy in the United States. It controls the amount of currency available in the U.S. by selling or buying back government bonds in the open market. It controls the amount of money commercial banks lend by raising and lowering the required reserve amounts. It affects the amount of money banks have to lend by raising and lowering the **discount rate,** the interest rate charged to commercial banks on money borrowed from the Federal Reserve System.

5. If the Federal Reserve Board raised reserve requirements for commercial banks, how would the banks react?

   (1) They would offer more loans.
   (2) They would extend less credit.
   (3) They would decrease their interest rates.
   (4) They would institute a Christmas savings plan.
   (5) There would be no change in bank policy.

6. The Federal Reserve decides that more borrowing will be good for the economy. It decides to

   (1) raise reserve requirements
   (2) raise the discount rates
   (3) buy back government bonds
   (4) lower interest charged to member banks
   (5) do nothing

7. The Federal Reserve System board of governors has seven members. They are appointed by the president, with the consent of the Senate, for fourteen-year terms. One member retires every two years. What can you conclude about the Federal Reserve System's role?

   (1) Its actions are dependent on the consent of the executive branch.
   (2) It is closely allied with the Senate.
   (3) The board of governors acts independently.
   (4) Each president has a lot of control over the board of governors.
   (5) Federal Reserve policy changes often.

8. Government bonds are "safe" investments. If a Treasury note is issued for ten years at an 8% interest rate, for whom is this a good buy?

   (1) a person who needs a fixed and regular income
   (2) a person who wants to get rich quickly
   (3) a person with outstanding debts
   (4) a person who wants to support the economy
   (5) a Federal Reserve Board governor

Before you take the GED Mini-Test, check your answers on page 125.

GED Mini-Test

14

TIP Try to answer a question in your mind before reading the GED multiple choices. When you have done this, then locate the choice that is closest to your thoughts.

DIRECTIONS: Choose the one best answer for each item below.

1. The government announced that it will not release funds for highway construction to New York City unless air pollution standards are met by a specified date. New York insists it must have the highway. What trend can you foresee for the city?

   (1) easier automobile inspections
   (2) more limits on car exhaust emissions
   (3) less emphasis on public transportation
   (4) more campaigning for industrial parks
   (5) expanding the Lincoln Tunnel

2. The Department of the Interior is responsible for the conservation and management of public lands, water and mineral resources, and fish and wildlife. With which of the following groups would you expect the Department of the Interior to be in conflict?

   (1) Congress
   (2) American Indians
   (3) the Sierra Club
   (4) real estate developers
   (5) mountaineers and campers

3. The Federal Government subsidizes farmers extensively. This contributes to the general welfare of the country by

   (1) making farmers rich
   (2) maintaining a steady supply of food
   (3) keeping people out of the cities
   (4) encouraging fewer people to be farmers
   (5) helping the U.S. to be "big brother"

4. Many citizens disagree with federal subsidies to farmers. They consider farmers to be

   (1) a special interest group
   (2) unnecessary
   (3) wealthy
   (4) lazy
   (5) unskilled

5. George Washington appointed a secretary of state, a secretary of the treasury, a secretary of war and an attorney general to help him to govern the U.S. In the late nineteenth and early twentieth century, the Departments of Agriculture, Commerce and Labor were established. Since 1950 Congress has formed four departments. These are Health, Education and Welfare; Housing and Urban Development; Transportation; and Energy. What conclusion can you draw from this information?

   (1) Federal understanding of how to maintain the "general welfare" has changed as society has developed.
   (2) Government bureaucracy is overwhelming.
   (3) George Washington was a good president; he did not need much help.
   (4) Society needs more control now.
   (5) The federal government is more limited now than in earlier times.

6. In 1965 President Lyndon Johnson created Medicare, a program that offers health insurance for the elderly. Currently the financial benefits for this program are no longer enough to insure adequate care for the eligible citizens. It can be concluded that

   (1) the government no longer cares about the elderly
   (2) there has been a rapid decline in the number of elderly citizens
   (3) there has been a dramatic increase in the number of elderly citizens
   (4) citizens should have a medical checkup yearly
   (5) no one can rely on government programs

Answers and Explanations

Practice *pp. 122–123*

1. **Answer:** (4) This is correct because it is Congress that has put into effect social welfare programs as a way of maintaining the welfare of U.S. citizens. Choice (1) is a power specifically mentioned in the Constitution. Choices (2) and (3) are not directly associated with Congressional activities. Choice (5) is associated with the Department of Defense.

2. **Answer:** (3) This is correct because those in favor of a protective tariff are the people who benefit by it. The protective tariff will make imported leather more expensive than locally produced leather, so local producers of leather, or ranchers, will benefit. Shoe manufacturers, choice (2), consumers, choice (4), and handbag manufacturers, choice (5), will all pay higher prices because of the tariff. Farmers, choice (1), is too general an answer.

3. **Answer:** (4) This is correct because you must look for an answer that increases revenue and cuts costs. Choice (1) cuts revenue and increases costs. Choice (2) cuts revenue and cuts costs, but you do not know from the information if the cost cuts are greater than the tax cuts. Choice (3) increases revenue, but also increases costs, so you cannot be certain that there will be a budgetary surplus. Choice (5) increases revenue by borrowing, which has a cost of interest payments, so the net result is an increase in costs.

4. **Answer:** (2) This is correct because losing American jobs and business is a direct effect of lack of protection for certain industries. Choices (1), (3), (4) and (5) are all opinions.

5. **Answer:** (2) If the reserve requirements are raised, the commercial banks have less money to lend. Therefore, they would decrease the amount of credit extended. Choice (1) would be difficult to do with less money. Choice (3) would lead to more people wanting to borrow money when the banks have less to lend. Choices (4) and (5) would not be effects of raising the interest rates.

6. **Answer:** (4) This is correct because lowering the interest rate to the banks would make it easier for the banks to lend money and for the average citizen to borrow. With choices (1) or (2) the banks would have less money to lend, so there would be less money to borrow. With choice (3) there would be less currency available and, therefore, less money to borrow. With choice (5) there would be no effect on the amount of borrowing.

7. **Answer:** (3) This is correct because in one term a president, with the Senate, can appoint only two out of seven members. Therefore, neither the president nor the Senate has a lot of control over the Federal Reserve Board of Governors, choices (1), (2) and (4). Choice (5) is incorrect because the fourteen-year terms for Federal Reserve Board members encourage stability in their responses.

8. **Answer:** (1) This is correct because this is the person who most needs a "safe" investment that will yield income on a regular basis.

1. **Answer:** (2)   From the information given, New York has two choices: provide its own money or comply with the air pollution standards. Stricter controls on car exhaust emissions would help to meet the air pollution standards. Choice (1) would probably increase air pollution by allowing cars that pollute the air to continue to operate. Choice (3) would probably increase air pollution by causing more people to use private transportation like cars, which pollute. Choice (4) would increase pollution because industry, even when regulated, always sends some pollution into the air. Choice (5) would probably increase pollution by bringing more cars into the city.

3. **Answer:** (2)   This is the best answer because it shows how help to the farmers improves the general welfare of the United States. Choice (1) is an opinion and is not supported in the item. Choices (3) and (4) are incorrect. Choice (5) may be a possible effect, but does not necessarily work toward the general welfare.

5. **Answer:** (1)   This is the best answer because you are asked to make a logical judgment on the information. The information states that more and more departments with specific duties were established as time went on. The logical conclusion would be that the government changed its interpretation of how it would best benefit the "general welfare." Choices (2), (3) and (4) are opinions. Choice (5) is a conclusion opposite to the one supported by the paragraph.

2. **Answer:** (4)   This question is asking you to determine who is against the Department of the Interior's goals of conservation and management of public lands. Real estate developers who want to build on the land would be against conservation. Congress, choice (1), established the Department of the Interior and decided its program. Choice (2), Indians, are protected by the Department of the Interior. Choice (3) is a group actively involved in conservation and, therefore, in agreement with Interior. Choice (5), mountaineers and campers, benefit from the public parks and recreation areas supported by Interior.

4. **Answer:** (1)   This is the most reasonable response because a special interest group should not be supported by the government under the "general welfare" clause of the Constitution.

6. **Answer:** (3)   This is the only logical conclusion. In the last few decades medical advances plus a better standard of living have helped lead to an increase in the number of elderly citizens. Choices (1), (2) and (5) are incorrect. Choice (4) is an opinion and is not a correct conclusion drawn from this passage.

The United States Today

The United States is a major economic and military force in the world today. It strives to find a balance in world power.

The United States was formed in rebellion against England. France gave the new country military and financial support. From the beginning the U.S. worked in an international arena; it balanced its own self-interest with the interests of other countries. It established trade agreements, friendships and alliances with foreign countries to help support its position in the world.

However, the United States was geographically distant from Europe and Asia. George Washington and Thomas Jefferson warned the people of the United States against "permanent and entangling alliances" that could prevent freedom and independence of action. There has always been a strong element of **isolationism,** or separation from other countries, in U.S. foreign policy.

As the United States grew larger and more populous, it developed a stronger economic and military position in the world. Historically, the United States has sought a balance among the strong powers of the world. The Monroe Doctrine established a protective American interest in the Western hemisphere. Participation in World Wars I and II led to a greater American influence in Europe and Asia.

Industrialization led to increased world trading of manufactured goods. The country's enormous resources of raw materials such as lumber, minerals and oil plus other non-manufactured goods led to its worldwide export trade. The economic interdependence of the United States and other countries is now firmly established.

Americans also feel a moral obligation to spread their ideals of independence and political freedom. Some foreign policy decisions are made to protect another country's freedom of political choice. Some wars have been fought to insure political integrity in other countries.

The United States' position as a superpower, along with the Union of Soviet Socialist Republics and the People's Republic of China, has created worldwide interest. First the **Cold War,** in which the free and communist countries engaged in indirect conflict rather than war, and now the era of **détente,** in which communication is increased in order to relax the enormous tensions between the superpowers, are major concerns of the nations of the world.

Identify Logical Fallacies in Arguments

This skill involves understanding and finding faulty logic and irrelevant evidence to prove or disprove statements.

To help identify fallacies or faulty logic in arguments:

Define the argument.   Is it chronological, sequential or based on cause and effect? Do the small details build up an inference, generalization or conclusion?

Check the accuracy of the information given.   If it is false or inaccurate, there is a fallacy.

Check the argument.   The facts *must* support or substantiate the argument. If the information given is accurate but does *not* support the inference, generalization or conclusion, there is a fallacy in the argument itself.

Examples

DIRECTIONS: Use the information on this and the preceding page to choose the <u>one</u> best answer for each item below.

1. Which fact does *not* contribute to the argument that there is a streak of isolationism in United States' foreign policy?

   (1) The U.S. is geographically distant from other countries.
   (2) George Washington warned against permanent alliances.
   (3) The U.S. grew larger.
   (4) The U.S. wants to preserve its independence of action.
   (5) The U.S. can be economically self-sufficient.

Answer: (3)   This detail supports the chronological argument that over time the U.S. has become more involved in world politics.

2. Which of the following campaign arguments would be used by a presidential nominee with an isolationist platform? The United States

   (1) should help other nations sustain political integrity
   (2) is economically interdependent
   (3) needs to help other Western countries contain communism
   (4) will be hurt by involvement with other countries
   (5) will profit by increased communication with other superpowers

Answer: (4)   This is the only argument *for* isolationism. All other choices are arguments for working with other countries.

Practice

As you read, ask yourself how specific information contributes to a general argument. Check your inferences by asking: Does this make sense? Is there enough support?

DIRECTIONS: Choose the one best answer for each item below.

1. U.S. foreign policy has sometimes been determined by a desire to protect another nation's striving for democracy. This desire would be a justification for intervening in

   (1) an internal political dissension
   (2) a dictatorship
   (3) a border dispute
   (4) a democratic nation threatened by external guerilla forces
   (5) a democratic nation's elections

2. Détente is a foreign policy that tries to relax tensions between the military superpowers. Which of the following would *not* be included in a policy of détente?

   (1) summit meetings
   (2) military actions
   (3) arms negotiations
   (4) diplomatic relations
   (5) cultural exchanges

Items 3–6 refer to the following passage.

U.S. foreign policy has developed as the U.S. government has defined different doctrines and plans for its interaction with other governments. The Monroe Doctrine of 1823 warned Europe that the U.S. would protect countries in the Western hemisphere against interference from European countries. The Open Door Policy of 1899 and 1900 called for open trade between China and all other interested nations. Franklin Roosevelt's Good Neighbor Policy established cooperation between the United States and Latin America. The Marshall Plan offered billions of dollars to war-torn Europe to finance its economic recovery after World War II. The Truman Doctrine of 1947 stated that the U.S. would help any government that requested assistance against communist aggression or subversion.

3. Which of the following influenced China's decision to allow Nixon to reopen diplomatic relations?

   (1) Monroe Doctrine
   (2) Open Door Policy
   (3) Good Neighbor Policy
   (4) Marshall Plan
   (5) Truman Doctrine

4. Which of the following contributed to Germany's strong economic position in the 1970s and 1980s?

   (1) Monroe Doctrine
   (2) Open Door Policy
   (3) Good Neighbor Policy
   (4) Marshall Plan
   (5) Truman Doctrine

GO ON TO THE NEXT PAGE.

5. Which of the following led to U.S. involvement in the war in Vietnam?

(1) Monroe Doctrine
(2) Open Door Policy
(3) Good Neighbor Policy
(4) Marshall Plan
(5) Truman Doctrine

6. Which of the following helped to determine John F. Kennedy's decision to demand that the U.S.S.R. recall its nuclear missiles from Cuba in 1962?

(1) Monroe Doctrine
(2) Open Door Policy
(3) Good Neighbor Policy
(4) Marshall Plan
(5) Truman Doctrine

7. Since World War II, U.S. foreign policy has been characterized by containment of communist expansion, deterrence of aggression and collective security in which countries band together to protect each other. All of the following actions are in line with this general policy *except*

(1) military treaties
(2) building of new weapon systems
(3) economic support for governments leaning toward communism
(4) expansion of the navy
(5) withdrawal from the North Atlantic Treaty Organization

8. The United States has a long history of friendship and alliance with the Philippines. For many years the U.S. supported President Ferdinand Marcos, despite allegations of graft and misuse of his office. In 1985 Corazon Aquino replaced Ferdinand Marcos as elected president of the Philippines. The United States' probable response was

(1) support for Mrs. Aquino and her government
(2) military intervention
(3) withdrawal of economic aid
(4) ratification of a new treaty
(5) closing of U.S. naval bases in the Philippines

9. Determination of U.S. foreign policy is shared by the executive and the legislative branches. The president appoints ambassadors, signs treaties with the advice of the Senate and is commander-in-chief of the armed forces. Congress has authority to declare war, ratify treaties and appropriate funds. This sharing of power is an example of

(1) democracy
(2) checks and balances
(3) law making
(4) theocracy
(5) diplomacy

10. The United States was a charter member of the United Nations, an organization that works for international cooperation. Since its founding in 1945, the members of the United Nations have more than doubled. Most new members are small developing third-world nations. This has led to

(1) strengthening of the international power of the U.S.
(2) greater public awareness
(3) disagreement between the U.S. and the majority of U.N. members
(4) withdrawal of the U.S. from the United Nations
(5) U.S. refusal to continue to host U.N. headquarters in New York City

Before you take the GED Mini-Test, check your answers on pages 132–133.

DIRECTIONS: Choose the one best answer for each item below.

Items 1–2 refer to the following definitions.

Many international political organizations exist. Below are five major ones.

United Nations (UN)—two parts: A **General Assembly,** where most nations of the world send delegates; and a **Security Council,** where delegates of the five major powers (the U.S., France, Great Britain, the U.S.S.R. and the People's Republic of China) meet.

North Atlantic Treaty Organization (NATO)— North American and Western European nations joined to protect themselves and each other against an armed attack against any of them.

Eastern European Mutual Assistance Treaty (Warsaw Pact)—The U.S.S.R. joined the Eastern European bloc nations in the Soviet bloc's equivalent of NATO.

Organization of American States (OAS)—Twenty-eight North and South American countries joined to defend each other.

European Community (EC, or the Common Market)—Western European nations joined to abolish trade barriers for a free movement of goods, services and capital within the EC.

3. President Jimmy Carter decided that a withdrawal of United States teams from the Moscow Olympics in 1980 would be powerful public evidence of U.S. moral disagreement with the U.S.S.R.'s

   (1) invasion of Czechoslovakia
   (2) non-participation in the 1976 Olympics
   (3) invasion of Afghanistan
   (4) poor wheat harvest
   (5) refusal to continue summit talks

1. The Cuban Missile Crisis of 1962 involved the construction of Soviet-backed missile bases on the island of Cuba. Initially the United States filed a complaint with an organization that represented the U.S. and Cuba, which ordered that the bases be disbanded. Cuba refused to comply and was expelled from this organization.

   (1) NATO
   (2) EC
   (3) OAS
   (4) UN Security Council
   (5) Warsaw Pact

2. The People's Republic of China has grown in power over the years. In the early 1960s China became a country with nuclear capabilities. In 1971 it became a member of the UN. If China and the U.S.S.R. were involved in a dispute over missile bases near their border, it would *most* likely be mediated by the

   (1) UN Security Council
   (2) UN General Assembly
   (3) Warsaw Pact
   (4) Common Market
   (5) North Atlantic Treaty Organization

4. The United States is a member of the North Atlantic Treaty Organization, or NATO. U.S. military aid would be called on by NATO in

   (1) a military conflict between France and Canada
   (2) a guerilla war in Mexico
   (3) elections of a communist government in Portugal
   (4) a U.S.S.R. invasion of France
   (5) a conflict between Poland and Hungary

GO ON TO THE NEXT PAGE.

5. Foreign aid is money, goods and services given to another country. Sometimes foreign aid is offered with no strings attached, as when a country suffers a natural catastrophe like an earthquake. Sometimes foreign aid is offered in exchange for something. For example, a country might be offered a missile system and defense training in exchange for U.S. rights to establish and operate a naval base. Which of the following truisms would a critic of the use of foreign aid as part of U.S. foreign policy use to justify his criticism?

(1) Do not look a gift horse in the mouth.
(2) Money cannot buy you friends.
(3) Birds of a feather flock together.
(4) A bird in the hand is worth two in the bush.
(5) Clothes do not make the man.

6. Part of U.S. foreign policy is to be informed about the military capabilities of other countries. Open, candid discussions can be held with allies, but information about countries unfriendly to the United States must be gathered in other ways. In 1986 two Titan 34D accidents happened, and the U.S. was unable to launch additional photo-reconnaissance satellites. This failure to launch the satellites will prevent the U.S. from

(1) getting additional information about economic policies in China
(2) tracking military deployments in the U.S.S.R.
(3) adding to their information about Western allies
(4) establishing naval sites in the Pacific ocean
(5) launching additional satellites when they are manufactured

Check your answers to the GED Mini-Test on page 133.

Answers and Explanations

Practice *pp. 129–130*

1. **Answer:** (4) This is the only situation in which a nation's right to choose democracy is being obstructed and, therefore, needs to be protected. National sovereignty, or the right of a nation to choose its own government, would keep the U.S. from becoming involved in choices (1) or (2). Choice (3), a border dispute, is a question to be decided by the two countries without U.S. interference. Choice (5) is an example of a country whose democratic process does not need to be protected.

2. **Answer:** (2) This would tend to heighten, rather than relax, tensions between powerful countries. All the other choices would tend to relax tensions and, therefore, would be part of a détente policy.

3. **Answer:** (2) The Open Door Policy, which protected trade between the United States and China, influenced the Chinese to respond favorably when Nixon decided to "re-open" the doors and re-establish diplomatic relations with mainland China.

4. **Answer:** (4) The Marshall Plan is the only choice that had an economic influence on Europe.

5. **Answer:** (5) The United States became involved in the war in Vietnam because South Vietnam was threatened by a communist guerrilla movement originating in North Vietnam. U.S. assistance was requested by the South Vietnamese government.

6. **Answer:** (1) The Monroe Doctrine, which established U.S. interest in preventing European interference in the Western hemisphere, was used to justify Kennedy's stand on the Cuban/U.S.S.R. missile bargain.

7. **Answer:** (5)   This is the only answer that would work against the policies stated. Withdrawal from a treaty organization would work against the goal of collective security. Choice (1) is in line with collective security. Choice (2) would be part of deterrence of aggression. Choice (3) would work against communist expansion by offering aid to countries that were leaning toward communism and, thus, encouraging those countries to consider the U.S. as an ally. Choice (4) would be in line with deterrence of aggression.

9. **Answer:** (2)   This is the correct answer because the Congress can act as a check on the president's foreign policy actions.

8. **Answer:** (1)   This is correct because Mrs. Aquino was democratically elected to replace Mr. Marcos. It is the only positive response that would express U.S. government approval of democratic change. Choices (2), (3) and (5) are all negative responses that would be used to express government displeasure and the U.S. approves of democratic change. Choice (4) is inappropriate because treaties are made between countries, and a change in governments would not require a change in treaty arrangements.

10. **Answer:** (3)   This is correct because U.S. policy as a major superpower is likely to be different from the foreign policies of many small developing nations. Choice (1) is inaccurate because the increase in number of members dilutes the power of the U.S. Choice (2) is irrelevant. Choices (4) and (5) are incorrect from general knowledge.

GED Mini-Test   *pp. 131–132*

1. **Answer:** (3)   This is correct because the OAS is the organization that deals with interests in North and South America. Although Cuba is a member of the UN General Assembly, it does not qualify for membership in the UN Security Council, choice (4). Cuba has never qualified for membership in choices (1), (2) or (5).

3. **Answer:** (3)   The U.S. would only have a *moral* disagreement about an invasion that violated another nation's integrity. Only the invasion of Afghanistan happened close in time to the 1980 Olympics. While the U.S. might be concerned about choice (5), it would consider that a policy agreement, not a moral disagreement. Choices (2) and (4) would not call for a foreign policy response.

5. **Answer:** (2)   The passage implies that foreign aid is used to encourage allies. A critic of the use of foreign aid would assume that money could *not* buy allies.

2. **Answer:** (1)   China, a major world power, joined the U.S., France, Great Britain and the U.S.S.R. in the UN Security Council in 1971. This organization would be the most effective in mediating an arms/border dispute. China does not qualify for membership in choices (3) to (5).

4. **Answer:** (4)   This is the only response that involved a NATO country under threat of communist expansion. Choice (1) is a conflict between two NATO members. Choice (2) involves Mexico, which is not a NATO member. Choice (3) would not be considered expansion since the government is elected by the people. Choice (5) is a conflict between two communist countries.

6. **Answer:** (2)   The main idea of the paragraph is getting information about military capabilities of other countries. Satellites that can take pictures from space would be useful for tracking military and defense changes in a country like the U.S.S.R. Choice (1), China, is presently getting economic assistance from the U.S. and would make necessary information available. Choice (3), the Western allies, would offer information openly. Choices (4) and (5) would not follow logically.

REVIEW
Political Science

In the political science section you have studied how the United States began its government, how government officials are elected and appointed, how the government is organized into the judicial, legislative and executive branches, and how the government has changed over time. The United States is a *democracy*, a government for the people and by the people. Consequently, it serves the general welfare, rather than special interest groups. It has established certain departments and agencies with specific programs to help citizens of the United States. It is also responsive to changes in the opinions of its citizens that are expressed through individual and organizational political action.

DIRECTIONS: Choose the one best answer for each item below.

1. The Agency for International Development is responsible for foreign aid programs. Much of the food sent to Africa and Asia to feed political refugees and people in famine areas rotted on the docks or in warehouses before it reached people who were starving. The *most* effective response of the Agency for International Development would be to

   (1) send more food
   (2) spray all foods with preservatives
   (3) offer technical assistance in food distribution
   (4) send money instead of food
   (5) refuse to send foreign aid to countries suffering from famine

2. Poor people are more in favor of social welfare than rich people. Laborers are more in favor of Medicare and Medicaid than business owners. Executives are more in favor of tax shelters than clerical workers. These statements show that political opinions reflect

   (1) self-interest
   (2) union viewpoint
   (3) educational training
   (4) sex
   (5) job status

Items 3–8 refer to the following definitions.

> The political opinions of individuals and organizations in the United States are ranged on a spectrum from radical left to reactionary right. They can be described in five categories:
>
> **Radical:** Advocates extreme political change, usually in a communistic or anarchistic direction
>
> **Liberal:** Relies on the federal government to solve big problems like welfare, medical care, unemployment, poverty
>
> **Moderate:** Looks for a pragmatic or practical approach, drawing from either a liberal or a conservative program, depending on the problem
>
> **Conservative:** Relies on local government rather than federal, believes the federal government has become too large and should take a hands-off attitude, supports private-sector involvement in social problems

GO ON TO THE NEXT PAGE.

Reactionary: Wants to return to society as it was before the government became involved, wants individuals to be responsible for themselves and for solving their own problems

3. A group that insisted that shelters for the homeless should be run by private individuals and organizations would be

   (1) radical
   (2) liberal
   (3) moderate
   (4) conservative
   (5) reactionary

4. What kind of organization would print a bumper sticker saying "Let's go back to the good old days . . . before the government took over"?

   (1) radical
   (2) liberal
   (3) moderate
   (4) conservative
   (5) reactionary

5. A person who voted a split ticket in most elections would be

   (1) radical
   (2) liberal
   (3) moderate
   (4) conservative
   (5) reactionary

6. Who would be willing to bomb a nuclear plant as part of a campaign to limit nuclear armaments?

   (1) radical
   (2) liberal
   (3) moderate
   (4) conservative
   (5) reactionary

7. What kind of organization would promote larger welfare programs and socialized medicine?

   (1) radical
   (2) liberal
   (3) moderate
   (4) conservative
   (5) reactionary

8. A politician who advocated a tighter budget, lower taxes and fewer government programs would be

   (1) radical
   (2) liberal
   (3) moderate
   (4) conservative
   (5) reactionary

9. In 1986, a non-presidential election year, President Reagan campaigned vigorously for Republican Senate and House candidates. "I didn't run to be a six-year president," he stated. He was indicating that a Democratic majority in the Senate and House would

   (1) support his political views
   (2) cooperate extensively with him
   (3) prevent him from accomplishing his goals as president
   (4) impeach him
   (5) pass a law shortening the president's terms of office

10. In 1986 the citizens of the United States returned a Democratic majority to the House and the Senate. Public opinion was indicating that

   (1) President Reagan was doing a good job
   (2) most people agreed with the president's new tax law
   (3) the Republicans were getting stronger
   (4) grassroots movements in politics were gaining power
   (5) the majority wanted a moderation of President Reagan's programs

Check your answers to the Review on page 157.

OVERVIEW
Behavioral Science

A New Year's Day football game at the Rose Bowl. Pasadena, California.

psychology
the study of personality development of the individual

anthropology
the study of the physical evolution of human beings and the cultural characteristics of particular populations or societies

Human behavior has been the subject of study from the time of the ancient Greeks. More recently human behavior has been studied scientifically through several disciplines in the field of behavioral science. These disciplines, or areas of study, include **psychology, anthropology, sociology** and **social psychology.**

Behavioral scientists study the development of the individual and the relationship of the individual to the family, culture, society and environment. They seek to understand the causes and effects of human behavior in biological, psychological, sociological and cultural terms.

Each group of behavioral scientists studies behavior through theories and concepts relating to that discipline, and their accumulated investigations have contributed vast knowledge to human understanding. Sociologists, for example, study the customs, values, attitudes and morals of different cultural groups. Some early sociologists tried to find the underlying principles that apply to all societies at varying stages of human development. But modern sociology relies more on statistical data, historical models and conflict studies.

Psychologists measure and analyze the differences in normal and abnormal behavior. Studies are frequently based on observation of human and animal behavior or on observation of whether behavioral changes are affected by environmental changes.

Social psychologists, as you might expect, combine some of the interests of sociologists and psychologists. Social psychologists are concerned with the influences of the group upon individual behavior. Thus, they study not only group behavior and the individual, but they focus on the interaction of the two.

Anthropologists are concerned with tracing the development of *homo sapiens* (the human race) to the present and with studying the artifacts of human culture as evidenced by language, laws, utensils and tools. As a result you will find that the two main divisions of this study are physical anthropology and cultural anthropology.

As you learn more about social and psychological issues in the following lessons, keep in mind concepts and principles of psychology, sociology and anthropology that will help clarify the nature of individual and group behavior.

sociology
the study of groups in terms of social relationships

social psychology
the study of the individual in relation to society

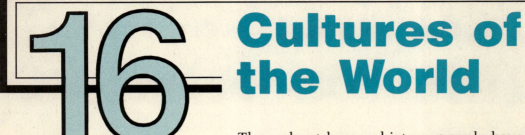

16 Cultures of the World

Throughout human history, people have adapted to their environment in order to survive. Once survival was assured, humans learned to use and change their environment to develop a culture. The **culture** of a region represents the knowledge, beliefs and customs shared by the people living there.

Different groups of people have developed different cultures. Cultures develop in a particular way in response to the physical features of the environment and people's interaction with other cultures.

Culture is a learned way of acting or behaving. Although a person is born into a specific race, for example, he or she learns to live and behave according to the acceptable ways, or **mores,** of the culture in which he or she lives. Over the centuries, people in different parts of the world have established unique cultures as seen not only through their music, art, architecture and trade but also through their ideas for living and shared rules of conduct that determine behavior and cooperation within that society. These ideas and rules are called **norms.** Differences in cultural attitudes and behavior are determined primarily by norms, mores and customs.

Religious beliefs often have important effects on the way people behave, on the size of their families, and even on what they eat and drink. The status of women often depends on social institutions that permit or limit social freedoms. The way children are raised reflects the predominant customs and mores of the culture. For example, the Chinese custom of ancestor worship emphasizes respect and honor for one's parents and grandparents. Young children learn to respect their elders because it is a cultural tradition. As a consequence, cultural influences are passed on from generation to generation.

As you read about some of the differences between Eastern and Western cultures, keep in mind that cultures are specialized in the way they adapt to their environment. The cultural differences between Western (America and western Europe) and non-Western countries (China, the U.S.S.R., India, Japan and Africa) can be seen both in the material aspects—such as clothing, tools, architecture and ways of making a living—and in social institutions—such as family, religion, government and community.

Identify Cause and Effect Relationships

A cause and effect relationship indicates how one thing affects another. A cause is what makes something happen. An effect is what happens as a result.

Writers often signal that a cause is about to be given. Some words and phrases that indicate that a **cause** will follow are:

because (of)	since	as a consequence of
as a result of	due to	reason

The following words and phrases signal an **effect**:

as a consequence	in order to	thus
as a result	therefore	so

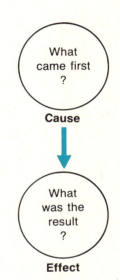

Look at the diagram at the right. Then try to identify the cause and the effect in the sentence that follows. The answers appear below.

Young children learn to respect their elders because it is a cultural tradition.

What came first?   the cultural tradition
What was the result?   respect for elders

Examples

DIRECTIONS: Use the information on this and the preceding page to choose the <u>one</u> best answer for each item below.

1. What is the *major* reason for human survival?

   (1) adaptation to an environment
   (2) development of a culture
   (3) interaction with other people
   (4) development of norms and mores
   (5) successful social institutions

Answer: (1)   Choice (2) is the result of choice (1), and choices (3), (4) and (5) are results of choice (2).

2. The effects or results of cultural differences are *best* expressed through

   (1) the status of women
   (2) clothing and tools
   (3) customs, norms and mores
   (4) ancestor worship
   (5) trade patterns

Answer: (3)   The question asks for the *best* way of expressing the effects of cultural differences. The other choices are simply aspects of a culture.

HINT ▷ When you study social studies, you need to know the causes and effects of certain events. While you are reading, ask yourself this question: Did the first thing really cause the second thing to happen?

DIRECTIONS: Choose the <u>one</u> best answer for each item below.

Items 1–4 refer to the following passage.

The first great civilizations of the world developed along the banks of great rivers. From the beginning, conditions in the Nile Valley in Egypt and Mesopotamia, in what is now the Middle East, were favorable for agriculture. It was in these river valleys that early people first worked out rules for living together in communities. The earliest rules dealt with irrigation. Cooperation was needed to build systems of dams and canals, leaders were needed to supervise the building and laws were needed to ensure fair use of materials and water.

The well-watered, fertile soil produced abundant harvests, which in turn made possible a large increase in population. As a consequence, cities and villages arose. So fertile was the soil of the Nile Valley that farmers could produce more than enough food for themselves and their families. As a result, surplus goods could be sold. This resulted in the development of trade and commerce, and with these came the exchange of ideas and inventions between peoples of different regions.

Since there was ample food available, not everyone had to be engaged in farming. Some people could develop arts and crafts. Potters learned to shape clay to make decorative vases; weavers learned to make fabrics and patterns of intricate designs; carpenters learned to build different types of furniture; and architects learned to construct elaborate buildings for government and worship. Thus, civilization and culture grew and prospered in the river valleys of the Middle East.

1. Which of the following tells why civilization first developed in the Nile River Valley and Mesopotamia?

    (1) It was a major center for trade.
    (2) The soil was fertile and produced abundant harvests.
    (3) The area had a large population.
    (4) People were deeply religious.
    (5) It was customary to live beside rivers.

2. Early laws were established as a result of the need to

    (1) build enough housing
    (2) limit surplus goods
    (3) create a just system of water distribution
    (4) govern commerce and trade
    (5) educate craftspeople

GO ON TO THE NEXT PAGE.

3. Which of the following explains what happened when people had enough to eat?

   (1) People from different regions no longer needed to communicate.
   (2) Farmers produced more than they could sell.
   (3) People moved from villages to cities.
   (4) People entered new occupations.
   (5) More people became farmers.

4. As a result of the growth of cities and commerce, which of the following *most* likely also occurred at that time?

   (1) Writing developed as a means of communication.
   (2) People lost interest in farming.
   (3) Explorers set out to find new lands.
   (4) Arts and crafts declined.
   (5) The Suez Canal was built.

Items 5–7 refer to the following passage.

A recent study by a Harvard-educated sociologist born in India sought to explain why poor people in India tend to have large families. As one illiterate laborer said, despite the fact that he has no land and very little money, he considers his eight children to be his greatest wealth. He says, "It's good to have a big family. They don't cost much and when they get old enough to work, they bring in money. And when I am old, they will take care of me."

Because this is a view that millions of Indians share, it represents a major obstacle in the effort to curb the rapid growth of India's population. The report states that "People are not poor because they have large families. Quite the contrary, they have large families because they are poor."

Some of the reasons that poor people are reluctant to reduce the size of their families relate to social customs that the Indian government is trying to abolish. The dowry system, for example, often forces a couple to try to produce sons to offset the economic liability they face in providing money to marry off their daughters. Many Indians think they must have eight children to allow for those who may die during youth and to ensure they will still have at least two adult sons to provide for them in their old age.

5. A *major* reason for the sociological study of India's poor was to

   (1) understand the reason for the size of their families
   (2) describe birth-control methods
   (3) describe the dowry system
   (4) explain why poor people live in India
   (5) caution people about overpopulation

6. According to the passage, many poor Indians do not like the idea of limiting family size because of

   (1) antigovernment sentiment
   (2) the country's low birth rate
   (3) the desire to marry off their daughters
   (4) social and economic customs
   (5) religious beliefs

7. Which of the following statements about India can be generalized from the passage?

   (1) The old take care of the young.
   (2) A large family costs too much.
   (3) The dowry system only produces sons.
   (4) Indians must have eight children.
   (5) Having children is a great wealth.

Before you take the GED Mini-Test, check your answers on pages 143–144.

PRACTICE   141

DIRECTIONS: Choose the <u>one</u> best answer for each item below.

Items 1–4 refer to the following passage.

An individual's personality can be understood as the distinctive way that person thinks, feels and behaves. Although each person is born with unique inherited tendencies that influence his or her personality, the culture in which that person lives may exert an even more powerful influence on the personalities of all people who share that culture. The process of sharing and learning that produces distinctive aspects of a society's material culture also produces distinctive psychological traits within the culture. Thus, behavioral scientists say that certain personality traits arise out of the individual's cultural conditioning. In other words, each culture produces certain typical personality traits. For example, in traditional Arab societies, most women behave in a shy and withdrawn manner, whereas women in some Polynesian groups tend to be socially more aggressive. Such personality traits are learned through life experiences shared within the context of family life. In effect, much of the way parents rear children is influenced by their culture; that is, their shared social ideas of the "right" way to bring up children.

1. According to the passage, what is the relationship of a person's personality to his or her culture?

   (1) Personality is one of the causes of culture.
   (2) The relationship between culture and personality depends upon the individual.
   (3) Culture is the result of personality.
   (4) Personality is one of the effects of cultural influence.
   (5) Culture has no influence on personality.

2. The Marquesan tribe of the South Pacific believes that prolonged nursing of infants makes a child difficult to raise. The Chencho people of India do not wean their children until they are five or six years old. What explains this difference?

   (1) Marquesan women do not know how to nurse.
   (2) The Chencho culture encourages prolonged nursing behavior in their children.
   (3) Marquesan women are more civilized and liberated.
   (4) Chencho women are born to be better mothers.
   (5) Climate differences affect how families raise their children.

GO ON TO THE NEXT PAGE.

3. According to the passage, the difference between the social behavior of Arab women and that of Polynesian women may be accounted for by

(1) cultural conditioning
(2) educational differences
(3) inborn personality differences
(4) geographic location
(5) the difference in climate

4. Which statement is *best* supported by evidence presented in the passage?

(1) Early influences on personality cannot be measured.
(2) Persons raised in the same culture eventually look alike.
(3) Polynesian women are bashful and quiet.
(4) Persons raised in the same culture tend to have similar characteristics.
(5) Many Arab women wear veils.

Items 5–6 refer to the following passage.

Social scientists have attempted to define several factors that are related to the national business cycles. They feel that, in a psychological sense, business cycles begin in people's minds. If people are optimistic, the economy expands and grows, leading to an upswing in the cycle. Initially, buying waves stimulate increased production and further consumer activity. Demand leads to supply. However, a national mood of pessimism can lead to an economic contraction and a cyclical downswing. Suddenly, having overestimated how much consumers will continue to buy, producers find themselves with surplus goods. The economy retracts as supply exceeds demand. Consumer activity lessens, and producers produce fewer consumables.

5. Social scientists feel that the major causes of business cycles are related to

(1) theories held by social scientists
(2) economic contractions
(3) overproduction
(4) economic upswings
(5) national psychology

6. Initial increase of consumer activity would *most* likely result in

(1) economic optimism
(2) overproduction and surplus goods
(3) decreased production of goods
(4) increased production of goods
(5) economic pessimism

Check your answers to the GED Mini-Test on page 144.

Answers and Explanations

Practice   *pp. 140–141*

1. **Answer:** (2)   The Nile River Valley provided fertile soil for abundant harvests, which favored population growth. This was a major reason for the development of early civilization in this region. Choices (1) and (3) are results (effects) of, not reasons (causes) for, the development of civilization in the Nile Valley. Choices (4) and (5) are not reasons for development of a civilization.

2. **Answer:** (3)   The last two sentences of the first paragraph state that the earliest laws were established to ensure cooperation in the building and use of irrigation dams and canals. These laws came before laws for housing, limiting surplus goods, governing, commerce and education.

3. **Answer:** (4)   The last paragraph states that when ample food was available, not everyone had to be involved in farming. As a result, new occupations arose. Information indicates the other answers are incorrect.

4. **Answer:** (1)   Although the passage does not say that writing occurred as a result of the growth of cities and commerce, it is the most likely response. Choices (2), (3), (4) and (5) are incorrect.

5. Answer: (1)   As stated in the first sentence (the topic sentence), the study sought to explain why poor people in India have large families. Although the article mentions the other responses, they are not the major reasons for the study.

6. Answer: (4)   As stated in the third paragraph, social and economic customs such as the dowry system and having at least two adult sons to support parents make limiting family size unpopular in India. The passage does not mention antigovernment sentiment, nor does it talk about religious beliefs in India. You can infer that India has a very high birth rate, so choice (2) is also incorrect.

7. Answer: (5)   Look for facts that support the notion that having a large family is a great wealth. See the first and last paragraphs that discuss the notion that children, not land or money, are a great wealth. Choices (1), (2), (3) and (4) are all untrue and not substantiated by facts.

GED Mini-Test   *pp. 142–143*

1. Answer: (4)   According to the passage, each culture produces certain typical personality traits. Therefore, it may be said that personality is one of the effects, or results, of cultural influence. Choices (1) and (3) are false cause and effect relationships. Choice (2) might be true, but the question asks for a relationship discussed in the passage. Choice (5) is incorrect, based on information given.

2. Answer: (2)   The differences between what these two groups of people consider the best approach to nursing imply that one culture values and encourages prolonged nursing while the other culture does not. Since, according to the passage, child-rearing practices are culturally influenced, the example given provides an explanation for these differences. Choices (1), (3) and (4) are opinions and are not based on any material presented in the passage. Choice (5) is not a valid inference.

3. Answer: (1)   The fourth sentence states that "certain personality traits arise out of the individual's cultural conditioning." Since education, as such, is not considered, choice (2) is incorrect. Choice (3) could be the explanation for the difference in behavior between two individuals, but the question deals with the difference between two *groups*. For choices (4) and (5), no evidence is presented.

4. Answer: (4)   The fifth sentence states that "each culture produces typical personality traits." Choice (1) is incorrect, as it is contradictory to the main idea of the passage. Choice (2) is incorrect, since the passage states that persons raised in the same culture eventually *act* alike, not *look* alike. Choice (3) is the exact opposite of what is stated. Choice (5) may be known to be true from your general knowledge, but there is no evidence to support it here.

5. Answer: (5)   The passage states that the psychological factors of optimism and pessimism on a national level are causes of the business cycle. Choice (1) is incorrect. Social scientists study, but do not create, the causes of business cycles. Choice (2) is the result of a national feeling of pessimism. Choices (3) and (4) are results, not causes, of economic optimism.

6. Answer: (4)   Consumer demand stimulates, and results in, increased production. Choice (1) is a cause, not a result, of consumer activity. Choices (2) and (3) are not an initial result of consumer demand. Choice (5), pessimism, is a cause of reduced consumer activity.

Shared World Problems

People of the world must cooperate to solve shared problems of the environment, energy conservation, overpopulation and human health and nutrition.

One of the major tasks facing world societies today is maintaining a healthy environment for living, working and raising future generations. The scientific and technological advances of civilization in the twentieth century have contributed greatly to prolonging life, reducing work efforts and providing leisure time. However, the very abundance of these advances has presented many societies with problems and challenges.

We are challenged with the necessity to maintain a clean environment as millions of cars and aerosol products emit harmful fumes, as non-biodegradable garbage and radioactive wastes become more difficult to dispose of and as certain chemicals have been linked to cancer and other disorders.

Energy conservation became a problem in the twentieth century as we became aware that the supply of fossil fuels such as oil and coal were limited. Industry and consumers must learn to use resources efficiently and to find alternative and renewable sources such as solar energy and the safe use of atomic energy.

As world population continues to increase at the rate of 93 million people a year, scientists estimate that by the year 2000, if food production has not increased sufficiently, the results may be catastrophic. Population control and better nutrition for Third World countries remains a major problem for this century.

Cooperating in finding solutions to shared problems will not be easy. Cultural anthropologists tell us that cultural values and beliefs of one group may blind its members to the values and beliefs of another group—values that may be equally worthwhile. These anthropologists have analyzed some of the ways different value systems can conflict with those of another culture when they interact. Some of these kinds of cultural interaction are **acculturation** (when a weaker group of people, brought into lengthy contact with a more powerful society, takes on many cultural elements of the stronger group), **cultural relativity** (the attitude that the customs of a society should be viewed in the context of that society's culture), **ethnocentrism** (the attitude that the customs of another society can be correctly judged in the context of one's own culture), **functionalism** (a theory that assumes that all cultural traits are useful parts of the society in which they occur), and **taboo** (the attitude that certain objects or people are forbidden because they are inhabited by a supernatural force and may cause harm).

Recognize the Role of Values and Beliefs

This skill involves identifying an author's prejudice, making a judgment about what is written and determining the accuracy of available data to substantiate conclusions.

Identifying an author's prejudice is not necessarily limited to those times when an author is being intolerant. An author's "prejudice," as used above, can mean his or her point of view or slant on issues or on life. For example, a poet, a farmer, a munitions manufacturer and a general might well have different **beliefs** about nuclear testing in the atmosphere. If each wrote a letter to a newspaper, the letter would be likely to reflect each writer's "prejudice"—in this case, their beliefs and values.

You will find that recognizing the author's **values** helps you to choose the appropriate answer to a GED test question. Keep the author's beliefs separate from your own. Do not answer questions according to what *you* believe, but according to what you understand to be the *author's* beliefs.

Example

DIRECTIONS: Use the information on this and the preceding page to choose the one best answer for each item below.

1. American nutritionists set up food programs to improve nutrition in technologically underdeveloped regions. This is an example of which definition?

   (1) acculturation
   (2) cultural relativity
   (3) ethnocentrism
   (4) functionalism
   (5) taboo

   Answer: (3) The diets of many primitive peoples may be good from a nutritional standpoint because of the inclusion of wild berries, roots, nuts and animal fats or hides. The insistence that an ideal breakfast exists represents an American, or Western, view of what is proper to eat.

2. Many African societies have adopted Christianity and Western beliefs, values and life styles. This is a process known as

   (1) acculturation
   (2) cultural relativity
   (3) ethnocentrism
   (4) functionalism
   (5) taboo

   Answer: (1) The process of borrowing the elements of a dominant culture by a dominated culture is known as acculturation. The dominated culture may identify with the dominant culture in the hope that it will share some of the benefits of the dominant culture.

Practice

HINT

When reading to recognize the role of values and beliefs in an author's passage, do not let your feelings about what you are reading interfere with answering the questions.

DIRECTIONS: Choose the <u>one</u> best answer for each item below.

Items 1–4 refer to the following passage.

In developing countries many women would bear fewer children if they had the knowledge and the means, and if it were culturally acceptable, to do so. "Imported" birth-control programs, however, are not the whole answer; studies show that such programs persuade only about 20 to 30% of the women.

Contraceptive technology is most effective when combined with social change. A recent report on 94 developing countries found that while the strength of a nation's family-planning effort was the single most important variable, fertility declined fastest in those countries that also had the greatest urbanization.

But social changes take time. It took all of human history for world population to reach one billion (in 1830). The second billion took only one hundred years. The third billion took thirty years, and when, in 1975, we reached the four-billion mark, only fifteen years had elapsed. If the fifth billion is reached by 1987, the elapsed time will have been cut to twelve years.

Such projections are based on the assumption that the basic energy, food and other natural resources required to support human life will be as available in the future as they have been in the past. The implications of the population growth problem touch upon virtually every other environmental issue. Nothing but the specter of war looms so large as a potential threat to humanity. No other human environmental issue warrants more attention.

1. The author believes that "imported" birth control programs do not work well because

   (1) women prefer to have large families for economic reasons
   (2) the programs do not reach the majority of women
   (3) at least 20% are using birth control
   (4) programs are not culturally acceptable to the majority of women
   (5) women already have birth control knowledge and means

2. What does the author believe accounts for the *greatest* decline in fertility rate in developing countries?

   (1) advanced contraceptive technology
   (2) social change and family planning efforts
   (3) the nation's family planning campaign
   (4) social changes in women's rights
   (5) the move to large urban centers

GO ON TO THE NEXT PAGE.

3. What is the main point the author makes in the third paragraph?

(1) Human history took billions of years to develop.
(2) Population is expanding faster than social change can slow it.
(3) In 1975 world population reached the four-billion mark.
(4) The author doubts that the fifth billion will be reached.
(5) The world population will continue to double every fifteen years.

4. The author believes that the issue of world population growth is second—or equal—only to

(1) the threat of world war
(2) the unavailability of natural resources
(3) unresolved environmental issues
(4) the need to improve contraceptive technology
(5) the problems of illiteracy and urbanization

Items 5–8 refer to the following passage and graph.

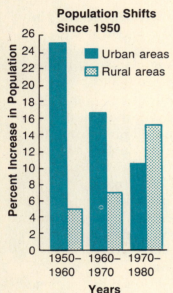

Population Shifts Since 1950

Percent Increase in Population

Urban areas
Rural areas

1950–1960   1960–1970   1970–1980

Years

Americans have always been a mobile people. From English settlements on the east coast to pioneer towns in the West, America, which had begun as a rural nation, became predominantly an urban one from the 1800s to the first half of the 1900s.

While some people were moving to cities, others began moving into suburbs. After World War II the suburbs mushroomed. During the 1960s the population of suburbs increased by 27% while the population of cities grew by only 6%. By 1970 more Americans lived in suburbs than in cities and rural areas.

Suburbs continued to grow in the 1970s, but a smaller proportion of the population lived in them. In the 1980s suburbs will continue to grow but at an even slower rate than in the 1970s. Despite problems associated with living in big cities, there is evidence that the population of cities is once again growing. American cities may be on the threshold of a rebirth as a new generation of urban pioneers reclaims its land.

5. According to the passage, Americans have always been a mobile people based on

(1) large English settlements along the east coast
(2) people moving from cities to suburbs
(3) the historical trends of population movements
(4) the aftermath of World War II
(5) pioneer settlements in the West

6. The author suggests that the trend of population shift in the 1990s may be

(1) a continuation of suburban growth
(2) a general population decline
(3) to rural areas
(4) toward living in cities
(5) along the Western frontier

7. Which of the following *best* describes urban pioneers?

(1) people who move to the suburbs
(2) people who move back to cities
(3) people who live in the West
(4) people who continue to live in cities
(5) people who live on ranches

8. According to the graph, the general trend of the population shift since 1950

(1) has increased in urban areas
(2) has increased in rural areas
(3) has decreased in rural areas
(4) increased most after 1970
(5) is the same for urban and rural areas

Before you take the GED Mini-Test, check your answers on pages 150–151.

GED Mini-Test

17

DIRECTIONS: Choose the one best answer for each item below.

Items 1–4 refer to the following articles.

THE RIGHTS OF FUTURE GENERATIONS

ARTICLE 1
Future generations have a right to an uncontaminated and undamaged earth and to its enjoyment as the ground of human history, of culture and of the social bonds that make each generation an individual member of one human family.

ARTICLE 2
Each generation, sharing in the estate and heritage of the earth, has a duty as trustee for future generations to prevent irreversible and irreparable harm to life on earth and to human freedom and dignity.

ARTICLE 3
It is, therefore, the paramount responsibility of each generation to maintain a constantly vigilant and prudential assessment of technological disturbances and modifications adversely affecting life on earth, the balance of nature and the evolution of humanity in order to protect the rights of future generations.

ARTICLE 4
All appropriate measures, including education, research and legislation, shall be taken to guarantee these rights and to ensure that they not be sacrificed for present expediences and conveniences.

ARTICLE 5
Governments, non-governmental organizations and the individuals are urged, therefore, imaginatively to implement these principles, as if in the very presence of those future generations whose rights we seek to establish and perpetuate.

The Cousteau Society

1. People lobbying for governmental control of pollution would be implementing which article?

   (1) Article 1
   (2) Article 2
   (3) Article 3
   (4) Article 4
   (5) Article 5

2. When Sweden monitored the increase in nuclear fallout following the Chernobyl nuclear accident, it could be said to have followed the guidelines of which article?

   (1) Article 1
   (2) Article 2
   (3) Article 3
   (4) Article 4
   (5) Article 5

GO ON TO THE NEXT PAGE.

3. Rachel Carson's 1962 best seller, *The Silent Spring*—a study of the dangers of pesticides then used in mosquito control and in crop dusting—is often cited for its influence on local legislation banning or limiting the use of DDT and similar pesticides. This cause and effect can serve as an example of which article?

(1) Article 1
(2) Article 2
(3) Article 3
(4) Article 4
(5) Article 5

4. A group of scientists is holding a convention. The topic of one meeting is "The Fragility of the Atmosphere: The Role of Scientists as Guardians." Which article *most* closely corresponds to the concerns implied by the meeting's topic?

(1) Article 1
(2) Article 2
(3) Article 3
(4) Article 4
(5) Article 5

Check your answers to the GED Mini-Test on page 151.

Answers and Explanations

Practice   pp. 147–148

1. **Answer:** (4)   Women in developing countries would use so-called imported birth control measures if these measures were culturally acceptable. The article does not provide information about choice (1). Choices (2) and (5) are contrary to information given in the article. Choice (3) is not a reason for the non-acceptance of birth control measures.

2. **Answer:** (2)   The main idea of the second paragraph is that fertility rate declined fastest in countries where family planning efforts are combined with social change. Choices (1), (4) and (5) are not specifically mentioned as contributing to the greatest decline in fertility rate. Choice (3) is just one of the reasons given for the decline in fertility rate in developing countries.

3. **Answer:** (2)   According to the information given in the third paragraph, population is growing by one billion in increasingly shorter times than social change can affect. Choice (1) is false based on your general knowledge that humans have existed for less than "billions of years." Choice (3) is a fact, not the main idea of the third paragraph. Choice (4) is counter to the author's position. Choice (5) is an erroneous inference; population is not doubling every fifteen years.

4. **Answer:** (1)   The second to last sentence of the fourth paragraph states that "nothing but the specter (threat) of war" is so large a potential threat to humanity. Although choices (2), (3), (4) and (5) mention important issues, none is as critical as choice (1), according to the author.

5. **Answer:** (3)   The entire passage traces population trends since the 1800s. Choices (1), (2), (4) and (5) are too specific and do not suggest that Americans have always been a mobile people.

6. **Answer:** (4)   The third paragraph states that there is evidence that the population of cities is once again growing, and that American cities may be reborn as new generations move in.

7. **Answer:** (2)   The third paragraph refers to urban pioneers as people who reclaim the land of the city, much as the original pioneers once claimed land in the West.

8. **Answer:** (2)   The graph shows that the population has steadily shifted from urban to rural areas. The population has increased, not decreased, since 1950, in rural areas, choices (1) and (3). The graph does not indicate a great increase after 1970, choice (4), nor does it remain equally divided between urban and rural areas, choice (5).

GED Mini-Test   *pp. 149–150*

1. **Answer:** (5)   Article 5 states that "Governments, non-governmental organizations and the individual are urged . . . to implement these principles."

2. **Answer:** (3)   Article 3 states that each generation should "maintain a constantly vigilant and prudential assessment of technological disturbances and modifications adversely affecting life on earth."

3. **Answer:** (4)   Article 4 refers to "all appropriate measures" including "research and legislation" to guarantee that these rights might "not be sacrificed for present expediences and conveniences."

4. **Answer:** (2)   Article 2 refers to each generation's duty "as trustee for future generations" to preserve the means of life on earth.

As you have seen, the behavioral sciences of psychology, sociology, social psychology and anthropology have provided us with information and insights into who we are and how we got that way. The study of individuals and societies reveals that we are both cause and effect of psychological and cultural determinants.

As you read the following passages, try to apply the strategies you have learned in assessing cause and effect and in recognizing the role of value and beliefs.

DIRECTIONS: Choose the one best answer for each item below.

Items 1–4 refer to the following passage.

Sociologists have classified the content of culture into material and nonmaterial components, and have used these concepts as the basis for theories of cultural change. The concept of material culture is clear: tools, artifacts and other tangible pieces of evidence that a culture produced. The concept of nonmaterial culture can be understood by thinking of it as everything we think and do and have as members of society. *Thinking* and *doing* and *having* are three important components of culture since they result in *ideas, norms* and *things*. Things, as you recall, are part of material culture and they are the result of thinking and doing.

1. What is the *best* statement of the main idea?

   (1) Sociologists disagree on the meaning of nonmaterial culture.
   (2) Nonmaterial culture means everything that is not material.
   (3) Sociologists have classified the content of culture into the components of material and nonmaterial culture.
   (4) Ideas and norms are part of nonmaterial culture.
   (5) Ideas and norms result in material culture.

2. Which of the following is the *best* example of nonmaterial culture?

   (1) pollution
   (2) the purchase of a car
   (3) Native American baskets
   (4) the change of clothing styles
   (5) courtship behavior

3. Which of the following is the *best* example of material culture?

   (1) adobe ovens for baking
   (2) religious practices
   (3) Hinduism
   (4) taboos
   (5) first-hand observations

4. Which of the following terms *best* describes "a culturally shared statement of how people ought to behave in particular situations"?

   (1) taboo
   (2) norm
   (3) idea
   (4) artifact
   (5) experience

GO ON TO THE NEXT PAGE.

Items 5–6 refer to the following passage.

The self-image of a child is based on patterns of child rearing. Although a child may be intelligent and physically capable, if reared by indifferent or abusive parents and subjected to constant criticism, that child may learn to see himself or herself as inadequate and undesirable. As a result in everyday life we see people who constantly underrate their own performance. On the other hand, we often see people who have a very exaggerated view of themselves. No doubt as children these people were surrounded by an admiring and doting family who praised even poor performance excessively. Some self-doubt and some ego strength are signs of a healthy self-image as we learn to be realistic about our strengths and weaknesses as adults.

5. Which statement below is the *best* statement of a causal idea?

(1) A child's intellectual and physical abilities determine its self-concept.
(2) The attitude of parents toward a child determines its self-concept.
(3) Admiring and doting parents are better than indifferent parents.
(4) Some people have a grossly exaggerated self-concept.
(5) Poor performance has negative effects on the parents' view of the child.

6. A person who constantly belittles his or her accomplishments unrealistically may have been raised by parents who

(1) subjected the child to constant criticism
(2) praised the child's poor performance
(3) ignored the child
(4) abused the child physically
(5) lacked education

Items 7–8 refer to the following passage.

Since it became universally recognized as a serious problem during the 1960s, the rapid growth of the world's population has fascinated anyone attempting to project the world of the future. Some observers have gone to bizarre extremes in an attempt to shock—calculating how long it would take humanity's total weight to surpass that of the earth, painting scenes of wretched masses shoulder to shoulder across the continent, or claiming that the world will begin to run out of food by the end of this century. Despite these impossible fantasies, population growth is a sobering and escalating phenomenon that promises to change the nature of life on earth if not dramatically slowed.

7. The author feels that the efforts of some observers to portray the world of the future are

(1) realistic according to experts
(2) universally recognized as wretched
(3) deliberately overstated
(4) disregarding the seriousness of the problem
(5) not going to change the calculations

8. The author believes that population growth

(1) was a serious human problem only in the 1960s
(2) is a fantasy of the future
(3) will be impossible to control
(4) will reach a limit by 1990
(5) may, over time, change how life on earth will be lived

Check your answers to the Review on page 158.

Answers and Explanations

Geography Review   *pp. 28–30*

1. **Answer:** (4)   Mountains are natural barriers to travel, but waterways help people to travel. Consequently, people settle along rivers and coasts. Choices (1), (2) and (5) do not pertain to the passage. Choice (3) is incorrect.

2. **Answer:** (2)   Major cities are found in lowlands and along rivers and coasts where travel is easy, not in mountains where travel is difficult. The implication is that facility in travel encourages people to settle and to spread their culture and ideas.

3. **Answer:** (3)   A tropical climate is a warm climate. The passage states that the heat of sun rays is greatest at the Equator. Therefore, the warmest climates are found close to the Equator.

4. **Answer:** (4)   Information in the passage indicates that elevation affects temperature. Of the choices given, only the mountains consistently have a higher elevation and a cooler temperature.

5. **Answer:** (1)   Latitude indicates location in relation to the Equator. Closeness to the sea affects evenness of temperature, choice (2). Elevation marks height above sea level, choices (3) and (5). Choice (4) is incorrect.

6. **Answer:** (5)   This is correct because it summarizes all the information in the passage. Choices (1) and (2) are contradicted in the passage. No information is given to support choices (3) and (4).

7. **Answer:** (4)   This is correct by finding the code for the greatest percent of exports (60+) and matching it to the countries listed. Only Mexico, of the choices mentioned, exports more than 60% of its total exports to the U.S.

8. **Answer:** (2)   The U.S. has refused to trade with Cuba since 1962 for political reasons. Fidel Castro, the communist leader of Cuba, encouraged the U.S.S.R. to send nuclear missiles to Cuba when Khruschev was in power and continues to support the spread of communism in other South American countries.

9. **Answer:** (2)   This is correct because Canada has the highest percentage of exports of the countries listed.

10. **Answer:** (1)   The map shows the percent of trade between Western hemisphere countries. Choice (2) is untrue. There is no information in the map about choices (3) and (4). Choice (5) is incorrect because of the amount of export trade.

11. **Answer:** (3)   Fossil fuels supplied 90% of energy needs in 1978 and are expected to supply 75% of energy needs in 2000. Other sources of energy will have to supply the 15% difference between 1978 and 2000.

12. **Answer:** (1)   The passage states coal demand rose as oil prices rose. The inference is that as oil prices drop, coal demand will drop.

13. **Answer:** (1)   The infant mortality rate indicates the level of health care in a country. Choice (2) is possible, but not the *best* answer because the passage states that geographers study human population for information about countries and cultures.

14. **Answer:** (2)   Political differences would result in borders being closed between adjacent countries. Choices (1) and (5) would not prevent nomads who remained nomads from following the routes. Choices (3) and (4) are not supported by the passage or by general information.

15. **Answer:** (4)   Federal appropriations have nothing to do with the physical environment.

16. **Answer:** (5)   The Asians eat rice as their staple food while Americans eat bread as their staple food. Choice (2), a factual statement, is not as specific or comprehensive a comparison as choice (5).

History Review   *pp. 75–77*

1. **Answer:** (5)   As large corporations reduced their fixed or overhead costs by producing goods in large quantities—mass production—they could offer the public newer and less costly products. This development helped the American economy.

2. **Answer:** (4)   Some large companies were guilty of exploitation of workers; by getting control of the labor market in some communities, large companies would then pay low wages and prevent workers from forming unions.

3. **Answer:** (2)   Antitrust acts such as the Sherman Act (1890) were enacted to regulate big business by breaking up monopolies and fostering price competition.

4. **Answer:** (3)   The Social Security Act of 1935 was passed after the stock market crash of 1929 and the Depression left people without jobs and money for the future. It has been expanded to provide medical coverage.

5. **Answer:** (1)   Amendment 1 provides for freedom of religion, but controversies such as state aid for transportation to parochial schools and prayer in public schools have raised this amendment for clarification in court decisions.

6. **Answer:** (2)   The Fourth Amendment, known as the "search and seizure" amendment, demands "probable cause" and specific warrants for persons and places to be searched and seized.

7. **Answer:** (2)   The Fifth Amendment prohibits the government from forcing an accused person to testify against himself or herself in one's own defense during trial. Testifying against oneself would be self-incrimination, which is thus prohibited.

8. **Answer:** (4)   The Fifteenth Amendment barred voting discrimination on the grounds of race or "previous condition of servitude," referring to former slaves and to blacks who were free before the Civil War.

9. **Answer:** (5)   The Nineteenth Amendment gave women suffrage—the right to vote in all federal and state elections. Prior to this amendment in 1919, only some individual states had extended suffrage to women.

10. **Answer:** (5)   The term "cold war" refers to political and military actions taken to prevent the spread of communism in the free world.

11. **Answer:** (1)   The veto power may be used by *any* of the five permanent members of the Security Council to defeat a Security Council decision. As noted in the passage, Russia has used the veto over 100 times, thereby limiting the effectiveness of the Security Council.

12. **Answer:** (2)   The beginning years of the New Deal were aimed at getting us out of the Great Depression. Problems in Europe, choice (1), were of no concern at that point. Choice (3) is incorrect because it was many years before the U.N. was to come into existence. Choice (4) is obviously incorrect because the U.S. was an Allied power, and choice (5) is incorrect because the Soviets and the U.S. were friendly toward each other.

13. **Answer:** (5)   The passage specifically states that, with the onset of the Cold War between the U.S. and the Soviet Union, Europeans began to worry about Soviet aggressive behavior. Choices (1), (2), and (3) were not at all related to the founding of NATO. Choice (4) was a separate occurrence that grew out of World War II as an effort to keep world peace.

Economics Review *pp. 101–103*

1. **Answer:** (3) External control would have to be exerted to stop spiraling wages and prices. Choice (1) would increase wages directly. Choices (2) and (5) would increase wages indirectly. Choice (4) might or might not affect the spiral.

2. **Answer:** (5) If you interpret the spiral correctly, labor wants higher wages and corporations want higher profits. Therefore, labor is against control of wages and corporations are against control of prices.

3. **Answer:** (3) Escalation of the wage-price spiral will definitely create higher prices.

4. **Answer:** (4) A centrally planned economy regulates both prices and wages.

5. **Answer:** (4) A baby-sitting co-op would exchange the service of baby sitting without the payment of any money.

6. **Answer:** (2) OSHA makes sure that safety regulations and practices are followed in the work place. Therefore, it protects the worker or labor.

7. **Answer:** (4) This is correct from the main idea of the text: Regulatory commissions support the general welfare over the specific welfare of an industry.

8. **Answer:** (3) This is a specific example of the regulatory commission's general activity of proposing and enacting rules for industries and then mediating in disputes.

9. **Answer:** (1) This answer follows from information in the text that regulatory commissions work for the general welfare of the consumer, represented by the public interest group, when it is being threatened by an industry, represented by the manufacturer.

10. **Answer:** (4) A regulatory commission interferes with the operation of the open market by intervening between the consumer and the seller. Choices (1) and (2) could be correct depending on the specific instance, but are not the best conclusion. Choice (3) is a possibility, but would not always be true. Choice (5) is incorrect.

11. **Answer:** (4) The government wants to protect American business, so the government will make it more difficult—i.e., more expensive—to buy Hong Kong radios.

12. **Answer:** (2) If more American radios were purchased, the problems faced by the businessmen pictured would not exist. Consumers would probably "buy American" if the prices were competitive with foreign merchandise.

13. **Answer:** (1) Cancelling tax deductions for sales taxes makes the actual purchase more expensive since there is no tax benefit. Therefore, people would buy before the end of the year in order to benefit from the sales tax deduction.

14. **Answer:** (4) Local television stations are in business to make money. In a deregulation situation they will look for an opportunity to increase their profits.

15. **Answer:** (2) The scarcity of fuel caused its price to rise steeply. All other choices are incorrect.

16. **Answer:** (3) Although the item remained the same, its cost more than doubled. All other choices are incorrect.

Political Science Review pp. 134–135

1. **Answer:** (3) This is the most effective way of getting food to people who are starving. Choice (2) is a possible solution, but not the most effective one. All other choices are counterproductive.

2. **Answer:** (1) The three statements are all examples of self-interest. Choices (3), (4) and (5) are possibilities from general knowledge, but are not supported by the information given in the text.

3. **Answer:** (4) Conservatives favor private-sector or local government solutions to social problems.

4. **Answer:** (5) People with reactionary attitudes want to return to society as it was before the government became so involved.

5. **Answer:** (3) Moderates choose political solutions from whatever program or party is most effective.

6. **Answer:** (1) Radicals advocate extreme political change. Bombing is an extreme action to attain a political goal.

7. **Answer:** (2) Liberals rely on the federal government to solve problems; therefore, a liberal would advocate larger welfare programs and socialized medicine.

8. **Answer:** (4) Conservatives believe in less government intervention, rather than more government intervention, in society.

9. **Answer:** (3) A president is elected to four-year terms, and Reagan expected to be president for two terms, or eight years. However, the president relies on Congress to help him legislate his programs. Reagan felt that a Democratic majority in the Congress would prevent him from reaching his goals as president.

10. **Answer:** (5) This is correct because it is the answer that indicates that the public wanted a change. Reagan was a Republican and wanted a Republican Congress to support him. Instead, the voters sent a majority of Democrats, who would probably differ with Reagan's programs, to Congress.

Behavioral Science Review   *pp. 152–153*

1. **Answer:** (3)   The two components of culture have been classified by sociologists into material and nonmaterial components. The main idea is stated in the first sentence and is supported by details throughout the passage.

2. **Answer:** (5)   Nonmaterial culture refers to ideas and norms, not things. Courtship, dating behavior, is an example of nonmaterial culture in many societies.

3. **Answer:** (1)   Material culture is best represented by tangible products, such as an oven made from adobe (mud) bricks for baking.

4. **Answer:** (2)   A norm is defined as a culturally shared statement of how people ought to behave in particular situations. Norms may differ from one culture to another.

5. **Answer:** (2)   A child's self-image is a result of (based on) the attitude and approach of those who reared the child.

6. **Answer:** (1)   You can infer from the information in the paragraph that people who constantly belittle their achievements were probably raised by parents who constantly criticized them as children.

7. **Answer:** (3)   The author notes that some efforts to portray the world of the future are "bizarre extremes" in an attempt to shock people.

8. **Answer:** (5)   The author states that population growth promises to change the nature of life on earth if it is not dramatically slowed.

Tests of General Educational Development

7 TEST BOOKLET NO. _____

8 TEST TAKEN AT _____

9 **TEST FORM**

TEST ANSWERS

DO NOT MARK IN YOUR TEST BOOKLET

Fill in the circle corresponding to your answer for each question. Erase cleanly.

MN ○
MO ○
MP ○
MQ ○
MR ○
MS ○
MT ○
MU ○
MV ○
MW ○
MX ○
MY ○
MZ ○
SF ○
SG ○
SH ○
SJ ○
SK ○
SL ○
SM ○
AR ○
AS ○
MC ○
MH ○
LR ○
LS ○

10 **TEST NUMBER**

① ② ③ ④ ⑤

	①	②	③	④	⑤		①	②	③	④	⑤		①	②	③	④	⑤		①	②	③	④	⑤
1	①	②	③	④	⑤	21	①	②	③	④	⑤	41	①	②	③	④	⑤	61	①	②	③	④	⑤
2	①	②	③	④	⑤	22	①	②	③	④	⑤	42	①	②	③	④	⑤	62	①	②	③	④	⑤
3	①	②	③	④	⑤	23	①	②	③	④	⑤	43	①	②	③	④	⑤	63	①	②	③	④	⑤
4	①	②	③	④	⑤	24	①	②	③	④	⑤	44	①	②	③	④	⑤	64	①	②	③	④	⑤
5	①	②	③	④	⑤	25	①	②	③	④	⑤	45	①	②	③	④	⑤	65	①	②	③	④	⑤
6	①	②	③	④	⑤	26	①	②	③	④	⑤	46	①	②	③	④	⑤	66	①	②	③	④	⑤
7	①	②	③	④	⑤	27	①	②	③	④	⑤	47	①	②	③	④	⑤	67	①	②	③	④	⑤
8	①	②	③	④	⑤	28	①	②	③	④	⑤	48	①	②	③	④	⑤	68	①	②	③	④	⑤
9	①	②	③	④	⑤	29	①	②	③	④	⑤	49	①	②	③	④	⑤	69	①	②	③	④	⑤
10	①	②	③	④	⑤	30	①	②	③	④	⑤	50	①	②	③	④	⑤	70	①	②	③	④	⑤
11	①	②	③	④	⑤	31	①	②	③	④	⑤	51	①	②	③	④	⑤	71	①	②	③	④	⑤
12	①	②	③	④	⑤	32	①	②	③	④	⑤	52	①	②	③	④	⑤	72	①	②	③	④	⑤
13	①	②	③	④	⑤	33	①	②	③	④	⑤	53	①	②	③	④	⑤	73	①	②	③	④	⑤
14	①	②	③	④	⑤	34	①	②	③	④	⑤	54	①	②	③	④	⑤	74	①	②	③	④	⑤
15	①	②	③	④	⑤	35	①	②	③	④	⑤	55	①	②	③	④	⑤	75	①	②	③	④	⑤
16	①	②	③	④	⑤	36	①	②	③	④	⑤	56	①	②	③	④	⑤	76	①	②	③	④	⑤
17	①	②	③	④	⑤	37	①	②	③	④	⑤	57	①	②	③	④	⑤	77	①	②	③	④	⑤
18	①	②	③	④	⑤	38	①	②	③	④	⑤	58	①	②	③	④	⑤	78	①	②	③	④	⑤
19	①	②	③	④	⑤	39	①	②	③	④	⑤	59	①	②	③	④	⑤	79	①	②	③	④	⑤
20	①	②	③	④	⑤	40	①	②	③	④	⑤	60	①	②	③	④	⑤	80	①	②	③	④	⑤

Permission is granted to reproduce this form for student use.

Instructions for Using This Answer Sheet

To be sure that your test results are properly scored and recorded:

- Use a soft lead pencil (not a pen) to mark your answers.
- Erase completely any errors or answers you wish to change.
- Make no unnecessary marks or calculations on this answer sheet or in your test booklet.
- Be sure the marks you make to fill in the circles are dark and fill the circle completely.

Do this: ●   Not this: ⦿ ⊗ ✓

DO NOT FOLD OR CREASE THE ANSWER SHEET.

In the time provided before you start the test, fill in the information in sections 1–10 on the answer sheet. In sections 9 and 10, be sure to write the letters or number in the box provided <u>and</u> mark the appropriate circle. (This helps avoid later scoring errors!)

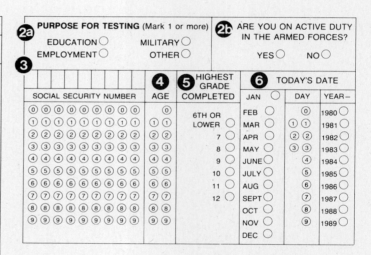

POSTTEST
Social Studies

TIP　Before you take this GED Posttest you may want to skim the test-taking tips presented in our program. Use them to remind you of ways in which you can help yourself pass the GED test.

DIRECTIONS: Choose the one best answer for each item below.

Items 1–4 refer to the following passage.

The Great Depression of 1929 to 1939 began with Black Tuesday, October 29, 1929. On that day New York Stock Exchange prices fell drastically as 16 million shares were sold. Later the stock market rallied, but business activity in the United States continued to decline. Too few people held too much of the country's wealth. Many ordinary people were unable to buy products that were manufactured. As manufacturer inventories mounted, plants closed and workers were laid off. As the number of unemployed rose, demand dropped. Even when goods were available, people could not buy them. Banks began to fail, and individuals lost their life savings, thus losing funds that might have gone into consumer spending. The industrial depression caused an agricultural depression since the unemployed could not even buy food. In California orange crops were dumped in the ocean because the cost of transportation would not be covered by the sale of the oranges. The poor starved while food was wasted.

1. According to the passage, one reason for the depression was

   (1) demand was greater than supply
   (2) supply was greater than demand
   (3) few people were poor
   (4) the dumping of the orange crops
   (5) many people were rich

2. What justification does the passage offer for the dumping of California orange crops?

   (1) People were starving.
   (2) There was an agricultural depression.
   (3) Banks were failing.
   (4) Shipping the crop was uneconomical.
   (5) The stock market failed.

3. Herbert Hoover, president in 1928, felt strongly that state and local governments, not the federal government, should provide relief for individuals who needed help. However, by 1930, 30 to 40% of the work force was unemployed. Private and local relief agencies could not deal with the massive demand for food, shelter and work. What might have been a solution?

   (1) relief from religious charities
   (2) raising import taxes
   (3) federal relief programs
   (4) local soup kitchens
   (5) a laissez-faire attitude

4. The Democrat Franklin Delano Roosevelt was elected president in 1932, primarily because Americans were dissatisfied with Hoover's response to the economic depression. Beginning with his inaugural address, in which Roosevelt promised "action now," he initiated the New Deal. At great cost to the federal government, FDR began work programs for the unemployed, "parity" pricing for farmers and relief programs. The long-term result of the New Deal was

   (1) greater popularity for the presidency
   (2) Hoover's leaving office
   (3) the U.S. leaving the gold standard
   (4) a depressed economy
   (5) greater federal power

GO ON TO THE NEXT PAGE.

Items 5–8 refer to the following passage.

World War II devastated the world economy. The cost of supplying the military and the destruction of the industrial cities and agricultural areas of Europe and parts of Asia hindered the recovery of the world economy. The United States, which was not economically injured by the war, took the lead in rebuilding the world economy. It initiated or participated in the following programs:

(A) The Marshall Plan supplied food and equipment to European countries in order to help them rebuild their economies.

(B) The Point Four program helps foreign countries to gain the technical expertise, or know-how, to develop their own natural resources and industries.

(C) The International Bank for Reconstruction and Development lends capital to countries or individuals for economically sound developmental projects. Many of these projects cannot get commercial loans at a reasonably low rate.

(D) The International Monetary Fund stabilizes the world currency exchange rates through international cooperation. Countries can buy or sell their own currency to the IMF in order to improve the balance of export-import payments.

(E) Military aid to countries allied with the United States and to countries threatened by communism.

All these programs together helped to rebuild the economies of the industrialized nations. All, except for the Marshall Plan, continue to develop the economies of the undeveloped nations of the world.

5. A small African country asks the United States for assistance in designing and implementing a fish farming cooperative. Which program will provide this assistance?

(1) the Marshall Plan
(2) the Point Four program
(3) the International Bank for Reconstruction and Development
(4) the International Monetary Fund
(5) military aid

6. A private investor in Bangladesh is sure that a jute factory would become self-supporting in five years. The investor has developed a financial plan, contacted buyers for the finished product and sellers for the raw materials and has gotten the support of local government. No Bangladesh bank will lend her money. Where could she get a loan?

(1) the Marshall Plan
(2) the Point Four program
(3) the International Bank for Reconstruction and Development
(4) the International Monetary Fund
(5) military aid

7. Why should the United States government finance the sale of American arms and weapons to the Middle Eastern countries that are fighting among themselves? This question is an argument against

(1) the Marshall Plan
(2) the Point Four program
(3) the International Bank for Reconstruction and Development
(4) the International Monetary Fund
(5) military aid

8. In 1964 the English pound was able to buy less on the world market and in England. To avoid devaluing the pound, England's Labor government borrowed several billion dollars to support the pound. From what organization did the English government borrow?

(1) the Marshall Plan
(2) the Point Four program
(3) the International Bank for Reconstruction and Development
(4) the International Monetary Fund
(5) military aid

GO ON TO THE NEXT PAGE.

9. Railroads expanded rapidly after the Civil War. In 1865 there were less than 35,000 miles of track. In 1880 there were 93,000 miles of track; in 1890, 166,700 miles of track. At the same time, Americans were inventing thousands of new machines to make work easier. In the 1850s the patent office issued about 1,000 patents a year; in the 1870s the patent office issued about 12,000 patents a year. By 1890, 25,322 patents were awarded. The rapid increase of railroad mileage and number of patents issued in the late 1800s were indications of the growth of the United States as

(1) an industrial nation
(2) a tourist country
(3) a political world power
(4) a democracy
(5) a nation of freedom

10. According to law, the House of Representatives has 435 members. These members are distributed proportionally among the states according to population. However, every state is accorded one representative, no matter how small its population. Even though Ohio gained in population between 1970 and 1980, it lost two representatives. How could this happen?

(1) The census figures were inaccurate.
(2) The gain in Ohio's population was at a lower rate than the gain in the country's population as a whole.
(3) The gain in Ohio's population was at a higher rate than the gain in the country's population as a whole.
(4) A smaller state wanted to change the laws.
(5) The House of Representatives refused to seat two members of the Ohio delegation.

Items 11–12 refer to the following cartoon.

"Are you sure you won't quit after a year or two to get married?"

11. The cartoonist is poking fun at an argument often used by corporations for not hiring a certain minority group. What is that argument?

(1) Men quit work to get married.
(2) Teenagers quit work to get married.
(3) Women quit work to get married.
(4) Men quit work to have children.
(5) Women quit work to have children.

12. In the 1970s and 1980s the government supported affirmative action programs. Affirmative action meant that companies not employing many members of minority groups tried to increase the proportion of minorities among their employees. The cartoon demonstrates affirmative action working for

(1) white men
(2) white women
(3) black men
(4) black women
(5) American Indians

GO ON TO THE NEXT PAGE.

13. Social scientists define an audience as a structured group of people coming together for a recreational or educational purpose. A crowd is a group that is less organized and may have only a short-term common interest. A mob is a crowd that finds a leader and turns to aggressive behavior. Which of the following would be a mob?

(1) spectators at a tennis match
(2) commuters stalled in a subway due to an electrical black-out
(3) people dancing in the streets at the announcement of the end of World War II
(4) a class on a field trip watching a play
(5) political protesters who attack police trying to keep order at a rally

14. A leader is a person who takes charge in a group. Some people explain the leadership role in terms of personality characteristics, but there are many types of leaders. Some are charismatic; some are administrative. Some are dictatorial; some are cooperative. Other psychologists argue that leaders are determined by the group situation, but often leaders are similar to their followers. With which of the following statements is the author of the above paragraph most likely to agree?

(1) The leadership role can be explained by personality characteristics.
(2) Leaders are charismatic, forceful types of individuals.
(3) There is no complete psychological explanation of why a person becomes a leader.
(4) Leadership is completely determined by the group.
(5) Leaders are very different from their followers.

15. Improvement in public health and sanitation and nutrition have led to declining death rates in many developing countries. The combination of continued high fertility rates and declining death rates in developing countries is *most* likely to lead directly to

(1) declining population growth
(2) increasing population growth
(3) increasing industrialization
(4) easier transition to developed country status
(5) decreasing improvements in public health

16. The Organization for Economic Cooperation and Development is the only international organization that includes all industrialized democracies. OECD countries have one-fifth of the world's population. They account for 80% of the world's trade. Which Asian country is *most* likely to be a member of the OECD?

(1) Indonesia
(2) Japan
(3) Vietnam
(4) Laos
(5) Thailand

17. Illiteracy is generally recognized to be an obstacle to economic growth and industrial development. Given that information, a developing country with an 80% illiteracy rate among adults, but a 10% illiteracy rate among high school age children would be *most* likely to develop what kind of program?

(1) port development
(2) building more schools
(3) farming cooperatives
(4) adult education
(5) small industry development

18. One unexpected result of the Spanish-American War in 1898 was that the United States acquired the Philippine Islands, Guam and Puerto Rico. One effect of the Spanish-American War was that the United States became a

(1) colony
(2) democracy
(3) monarchy
(4) English-speaking country
(5) colonizing power

GO ON TO THE NEXT PAGE.

Items 19–22 refer to the following map.

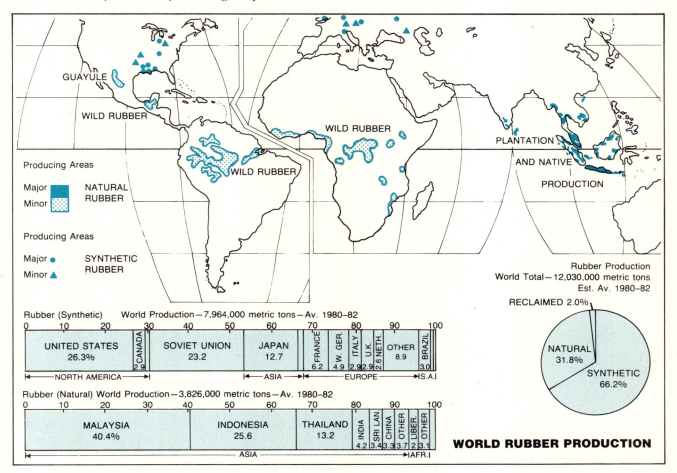

WORLD RUBBER PRODUCTION

19. From the information on the map, what kind of climate is necessary to grow rubber?

   (1) polar
   (2) temperate
   (3) mild
   (4) tropical
   (5) dry

20. From the information on the map, which country is probably the world's major producer of synthetic rubber?

   (1) France
   (2) Japan
   (3) United States
   (4) U.S.S.R.
   (5) West Germany

21. Rubber is vital to the production of tanks, airplanes and other military vehicles used in conventional warfare. The *best* explanation for why the U.S.A. and U.S.S.R. are major producers of synthetic rubber is that these countries

   (1) are major military powers
   (2) have no natural rubber plantations
   (3) are engaged in a cold war
   (4) recognize the need for a local source of rubber in case they must fight a conventional war
   (5) have the capital and industrial resources necessary to support synthetic rubber production

22. According to the map, which area of the world is the major natural rubber producer?

   (1) Africa
   (2) Asia
   (3) Europe
   (4) North America
   (5) South America

Answers and Explanations

Social Studies Posttest *pp. 161–165*

1. **Answer:** (2) This is correct because the passage states that ordinary people were unable to buy (demand was low) and inventories mounted (supply was high). Choice (1) is the opposite of the situation; choice (3) is contradicted in the paragraph; choice (4) is a result, not a reason; choice (5) is contradicted in the paragraph.

2. **Answer:** (4) This is correct because the passage states that the market price for the oranges would not pay for the cost of transportation; therefore, shipping the crop was uneconomical. Choices (1), (2), (3) and (5) are facts mentioned in the passage, but are not justifications for dumping the crops.

3. **Answer:** (3) This choice would have been a solution because the federal government had greater resources available. Choices (1) and (4) are wrong because the item states that private and local relief agencies were inadequate. Choice (2) would make it more difficult to buy imported goods, but would not affect most people who had no money even to buy necessities. Choice (5) means that the government would do nothing to break the cycle of depression; therefore, it is not a solution.

4. **Answer:** (5) This is correct because during the New Deal the federal government took to itself many functions that it had not had before. Those functions continue to be filled by the federal government. Choice (1) is an opinion; choice (2) is not a result since it occurred before the New Deal; choice (3) is not indicated in the passage; choice (4) was true before the New Deal, not after.

5. **Answer:** (2) This is correct because the Point Four program provides technical assistance that is needed in order to begin the fish farm cooperative.

6. **Answer:** (3) This is correct because private individuals who need capital assistance for development projects can get loans from the International Bank for Reconstruction and Development.

7. **Answer:** (5) This is correct because the question concerns the sale of arms and weapons.

8. **Answer:** (4) This is correct because the International Monetary Fund is concerned with the stabilization of currency.

9. **Answer:** (1) This is correct because both the expansion of the railroads and the increase in inventions indicate that the country was developing industrially. Choice (2) is wrong: railroads might be used for tourism, but inventions would not. Choice (3) is incorrect. Neither the railroads nor the inventions are directly associated with political or world power. Choices (4) and (5) are incorrect because the railroads and the number of inventions do not influence democracy or freedom.

10. **Answer:** (2) This is correct from the information in the paragraph. Representatives are distributed proportionally, so proportionally the Ohio population went down. Therefore, it must have gained population more slowly than the rest of the country. Choice (1) is an opinion with no support in the item; choice (3) would have increased the number of Ohio representatives; choice (4) is not supported and would not be possible; choice (5) is not supported.

11. **Answer:** (3)   This is correct from the caption. The role reversal here works so that the woman asks the man the question women were often asked: "Are you going to quit to get married?" The argument was not that men quit work to get married, but that women quit work to get married. Choice (2) is incorrect because there is no clear indication that a teenager is involved. Choices (4) and (5) are incorrect because there is no reference to having children in the caption.

13. **Answer:** (5)   This is correct because it meets the definition offered for a mob: a crowd of political protesters turned to aggressive action. Choices (1) and (4) are audiences; choices (2) and (3) are crowds.

15. **Answer:** (2)   This is the correct answer because it is the *direct* result of fewer deaths and more or equal number of births. Choice (1) is the opposite of what would happen. Choices (3)–(5) are possible *indirect* results.

17. **Answer:** (4)   This is the best answer because the illiteracy rate is very high among adults but relatively low among the school age children. Adult education would be more effective in attacking the illiteracy rate than building new schools, choice (2). No information is given in the item to suggest whether the country even has a port, choice (1), is primarily agricultural, choice (3), or needs small industry, choice (5).

19. **Answer:** (4)   This is correct because all the areas that produce natural rubber are very close to the Equator and, therefore, have a tropical climate.

21. **Answer:** (4)   This is the best answer because it links information from the map (the U.S. and U.S.S.R. have no natural rubber sources) and information from the item (rubber is necessary in conventional warfare). Choices (1) to (3) and (5) are all true, but are not the best explanations.

12. **Answer:** (2)   The cartoon uses role reversal to make its point; instead of a man hiring a woman, a woman in personnel is hiring a man. The woman has the benefit of affirmative action because she has been hired in a management position. White men, choice (1), is the only group that did not need the benefit of affirmative action. Choices (3) to (5) are not pictured in the cartoon.

14. **Answer:** (3)   This is correct because the writer is dissatisfied with both the personality and the group explanation of the leadership role. Choice (1) is argued against by the paragraph. Choice (2) is only one kind of leader. Choice (4) is argued against by the writer. Choice (5) is contradicted in the paragraph.

16. **Answer:** (2)   This is the correct answer because Japan is the only country listed that fits both parts of the membership requirement: It is a democracy, and it is industrialized. Choices (3) and (4) are not democracies; choices (1) and (5) are not industrialized nations.

18. **Answer:** (5)   In 1898 the U.S.A. was no longer a colony, choice (1). It has never been a monarchy, choice (3). Since it attained freedom it has always been choices (2) and (4). The only possible answer is choice (5), that the U.S. became a colonizing power because the countries mentioned were treated as colonies by the U.S.

20. **Answer:** (3)   This is correct from information in the legend. The United States has seven major and three minor synthetic rubber producing areas, the most of any country listed.

22. **Answer:** (2)   This is correct from the legend. The concentration of major natural rubber producers is in Asia.

Pretest/Posttest Diagnostic Chart

For the Pretest After you check your answers, look at the chart below. Circle the number of each problem you missed. Find the skills in which you need the most help. Then find those skills listed in the Table of Contents and begin your studying in those skill areas.

For the Posttest After you check your answers, look at the chart below. Circle the number of each problem you missed. Find the skills in which you still need help. Then find those skills listed in the Table of Contents and review those skill areas, paying special attention to the Strategies for Reading pages and the Answers and Explanations pages for the Practice items and the GED Mini-Test.

CONTENT AREAS

SKILLS	Geography Pretest	Geography Posttest	History Pretest	History Posttest	Economics Pretest	Economics Posttest	Political Science Pretest	Political Science Posttest	Behavioral Science Pretest	Behavioral Science Posttest
Restate Information			1	2, 8		5	18			13
Identify Implications	21, 23		4	4	14			10		12
Use Given Ideas in Another Context	24				12	7			5, 6, 7, 8, 9, 10	14
Distinguish Conclusions from Supporting Statements			2	3	20			1		
Identify Cause and Effect Relationships				9	11, 15, 16					15
Recognize Unstated Assumptions	22	21	3, 13				25, 26	18		11
Assess the Adequacy of Data to Support Conclusions		19, 20, 22				16, 17	19	6	17	

Index